凝視　齊柏林：台灣的四維空間

In Focus : Chi Po Lin and Taiwan's Four-Dimensional Spacetime

In Focus
Chi Po Lin

出 版 者 的 話

A Word from the Publisher

向不朽的精神與貢獻致敬　　　　　　　　　　　　歐 晉 德　　006
／向齊柏林致敬

Paying Homage to Chi Po-lin's　　　　　　　　　　Ou Chin-der
Contributions and Immortal Spirit

作 者 的 話

Author's Remarks

好好愛護腳下這片土地　　　　　　　　　　　　　齊 柏 林　　008

Please Cherish This Land That Is Our Home　　　　Chi Po-lin

推 薦 序

Forewords

看見台灣，看見齊柏林　　　　　　　　　　　　　蕭 瓊 瑞　　012
Seeing Taiwan, Seeing Chi Po-lin　　　　　　　　Hsiao Chong-ray

一位理性與情感兼俱的空中攝影家　　　　　　　　林 志 明　　016
An Aerial Photographer both Rational and Sensitive　Lin Chi-ming

昨日仍然美麗與驚歎　　　　　　　　　　　　　　劉 克 襄　　020
Yesterday, Marvelous and Beautiful　　　　　　　Liu Ke-xiang

我們不會再有第二個齊柏林　　　　　　　　　　　陳 文 茜　　024
There Will Be No Second Chi Po-lin　　　　　　　Sisy Chen

生命是能夠相互感知的集合體　　　　　　　　　　李 家 維　　026
Life Is a Collective Whose Parts Are　　　　　　　Li Chia-wei
Capable of Mutual Understanding and Feeling

凝視　　　　　　　　　　　　　　　　　　　　　黃 寶 琴　　030
In Focus　　　　　　　　　　　　　　　　　　　Huang Pao-chin

前 導　夢 想 的 起 點

Preface　The Starting Point of Dreams　033

自 然 的 器 度

The Elegance of Nature　069

生 命 的 廣 度

The Breadth of Life　127

土 地 的 溫 度

The Warmth of the Land　171

和 諧 的 限 度

The Limits of Harmony　195

最後的凝視　205
The Last Gaze

看見・齊柏林基金會介紹　213
Chi Po-lin Foundation

齊柏林空間介紹
Chi Po-lin Museum

齊柏林年表　214
Chi Po-lin: Timeline

大霸尖山、雪山主峰——聖稜線
Mt. Dabajian, Mt. Xue - the Holy Ridge
新竹、苗栗 Hsinchu and Miaoli 2010

大霸尖山聳立於雪山山脈北端，有「世紀奇峰」
美名，泰雅族和賽夏族均視為聖山，其與台灣第
二高峰雪山主峰之間的山脊連峰，更是山岳界馳
名的縱走挑戰路線「聖稜線」。

Mt. Dabaijian sits at the northern end of the Mt. Xue
Range. Known as "the peak of a century," it is regarded
as a holy mountain by the Atayal and the Saisiyat. The
ridge between it and Mt. Xue's main peak, which is the
second highest in Taiwan, is the challenging Holy Ridge
that is renowned among Taiwan's climbing community.

向不朽的精神與貢獻致敬 / 向齊柏林致敬

齊柏林，一個生命的勇者、一位台灣土地上高品格的人物、我們大家共同的好朋友！

在齊柏林短暫的一生當中，他把最精華的歲月都奉獻給了台灣這塊土地，他用他的熱情、專業、堅持和毅力，勇敢並義無反顧地飛在高空之上，為我們記錄自然與生命演出的每一刻悸動，為我們見證土地與環境變遷的每一段故事。

除了以金馬獎最佳紀錄片《看見台灣》引領我們省思台灣的美麗與哀愁，齊柏林投入近 25 載寒暑，在空中飛行超過 2500 個小時，累積 10 多萬張底片、20 多萬張數位照片，以及無數影片素材，為我們留下了記錄台灣土地與環境脈動極其珍貴的影像資產，不只無可取代，而且也絕不可能重來！

為了感念齊柏林「看見台灣，守護家園」的職志與精神，為了延續他對台灣土地與環境的愛及關懷，我們在 2018 年成立了「看見‧齊柏林基金會」，我們也接續在 2019 年設立了「齊柏林空間」，希望能夠建構一個築夢平台，並凝聚社會上更多的資源與力量，大家一起攜手協力，在齊柏林的心血基礎上來推動環境教育，繼續深耕台灣土地、環境與生命關懷的議題，讓台灣凝聚更多正向的力量，讓台灣更美、更好，讓台灣不斷被世界看見！

本書《凝視 齊柏林：台灣的四維空間》，以摘要方式彙集齊柏林空拍作品所涉獵的多元面向，看見齊柏林追求夢想的起源與啟發：自然的器度單元，看見齊柏林巡禮台灣地景的無限風華；生命的廣度單元，看見齊柏林眷顧台灣人民營生的居住環境；土地的溫度單元，看見齊柏林詠讚台灣豐饒大地以及勤奮人民的互動；和諧的限度單元，看見齊柏林揭露台灣重大事件的真實面容。誠屬齊柏林以空拍闡述台灣生命故事的精彩縮影。

本書付梓發行，有賴許多熱心朋友鼎力襄助，在急迫又有限的時程內順利達成任務，併此銘謝，也希望透過本書一幀幀空拍影像的呈現，讓大家對我們共同生活的這塊土地樣貌，獲致更多不同層面的體悟和認識，爰以為序。

看見‧齊柏林基金會 董事長

（簽名） 謹識

Paying Homage to Chi Po-lin's Contributions and Immortal Spirit

Chi Po-lin lived a courageous, noble life. He benefitted Taiwan immensely and was a friend to everyone.

He gave the crucial years of his short life to this land, demonstrating great passion, professionalism, determination and perseverance. With a great sense of duty and without a second thought for his own safety, he flew many times over Taiwan's natural landscapes, documenting the story—vibrant moment by vibrant moment, chapter by chapter—of the island's evolving natural environment.

He is well known for his Golden Horse-winning documentary *Beyond Beauty: Taiwan from Above*, which put the spotlight on the beauty and sorrows of Taiwan's natural environment. But his work didn't stop there: Chi Po-lin spent more than 2,500 hours airborne over a span of nearly 25 years, accumulating more than 100,000 negatives, 200,000 digital photographs, and countless video clips. These rich photographic resources are irreplaceable. Nothing like them will ever appear again.

The Chi Po-lin Foundation was established in 2018 to remember Chi Po-lin's spirit and to push toward the goal of "observing and protecting his homeland of Taiwan." We then followed up by launching the Chi Po-lin Museum Project. Our goal there is to build a platform for launching his dreams and to direct more of society's resources toward building on the foundation that Chi Po-lin laid, thus promoting environmental education and examining in depth the issues that are related to the natural environment and life here. And with that, Taiwan may gather only more positive energy, so it can continually grow better and more beautiful as its profile rises in the world!

In Focus: Chi Po-lin and Taiwan's Four-Dimensional Spacetime collects some of Chi's best photographs, which are matched with short passages of text explaining them. The book captures his work in all its glorious diversity. We see the source and inspiration for Chi Po-lin's dream. In the "Elegance of Nature" section, Chi's unabated drive to capture the beauty of Taiwan's landscapes is on full display. In the "Breadth of Life" section, one sees his concern for the environments in Taiwan where people live and work. In the "Warmth of the Land" section, we see him paying homage to the interaction between Taiwan's rich natural resources and its hard-working people. In the "Limits of Harmony" section, we see how Chi Po-lin exposes the truth about incidents of environmental destruction in Taiwan. Taken together, the photos in the collection serve as an honest encapsulation of Chi Po-lin's efforts to describe Taiwan's evolving story from the air.

To bring this work to completion, we have relied on the help of many enthusiastic friends, who smoothly achieved their missions in the face of tight time constraints. Thanks to their efforts, we can present this book as framework through which all of us can see images of this land we love, and through them gain new perspectives and understandings of it.

Chairman of the Chi Po-lin Foundation   Ou Chin-der

好好愛護腳下這片土地

齊柏林

二十多年來，我跟著直升機飛上天空，拍遍台灣各個角落，有山，有河，有海，有城市，從天空看自己生活過的土地著實是一項很迷人的工作。

曾經很多人問我：拍遍台灣每個角落，到底什麼地方最美？我的回答總是：「只要沒有人的地方，就是最美、最漂亮的地方。」

有一次難忘的經驗是在棲蘭山拍攝時，緩緩降低高度的直升機旋翼擾動了周遭的空氣，霎時把帶有森林味道的氣息不斷往機艙裡送；那股清甜的味道融合了原始森林裡淡淡的檜木香氣，我從來沒聞過這樣的味道，也因為空氣太清新了，有抽菸習慣的飛行員呼氣時的煙味，頓時變得格外明顯。

然而，隨著氣候愈來愈極端、劇烈地變化，發生在土地上的災難規模也隨之愈加巨大，更令人感慨的是，我們只記得災難來臨時的慘烈狀況，卻從未從頭去細究：何以災難會發生？我提醒自己絕不能袖手旁觀，並且意識到唯一能做的，就是透過每一次飛行所記錄的影像，把親眼見到的一切，送到大家的眼前。

到了後期，我不再追求拍攝美麗的事物，在按下快門時每個念頭想的，都是希望能為土地做些記錄；我深深覺得，記錄工作的意義不僅是單純記錄台灣這片土地的景色、樣貌，還要能進一步去觀察和警戒環境災難。

很多人都說台灣很小，還有什麼好記錄的嗎？我總會反問：「那麼你都看過了嗎？又了解多少呢？」

確實，真實世界裡「美麗中總是帶著缺憾」。透過鏡頭我想告訴你的是，無論在這片土地上發生過美好的、不美好的事跡，都是在提醒我們好好愛護自己腳下這片土地。

看見・齊柏林基金會編輯部 摘錄

Please Cherish This Land That Is Our Home

For more than 20 years, I've climbed into helicopters to take aerial photographs of Taiwan—its mountains, its rivers, its coastal waters, its cities…. To be employed to look down from the air upon the place where I live my life is captivating work indeed!

Many people have asked me: After having taken photographs of Taiwan from so many different angles, which of its places do I find most beautiful? My answer is always: The prettiest places are the places with no people.

One unforgettable memory I have is of photographing Mt. Qilan. As the helicopter slowly descended, it stirred up the air nearby, bringing the fragrance of the forest into the helicopter's cabin. That gust of clean, sweet air carried with it a faint scent of the Chinese junipers that are native to those forests. I had never smelled that scent before, and because it was so fresh, the tobacco smell on the breath of the pilot, who was a smoker, suddenly became that much more distinct.

Yet with climate change causing ever-more-extreme weather, the scope of natural disasters occurring on this land are likewise growing. Regrettably, we only remember the desperate situations that occur after the disasters have arrived, but never go back to ask the question: Why, ultimately, did the disasters happen? I have reminded myself not to simply stand by and do nothing. Furthermore, I have realized that what I can do is to record everything I see with my own eyes and then show those records to everyone.

More recently, I no longer seek out beautiful vistas. Rather, while clicking my camera's shutter, I have been aiming to make a record of the land. I deeply feel that the meaning in documentary photography is not found merely in recording scenic vistas; it is even more important to advance to observations and warnings about environmental disasters.

Many people ask: Since Taiwan is so small, how can there be much to document? I always respond: So have you seen it all? How much do you understand about it?

Indeed, in the real world, "beauty always comes with regret." Here is what I want to tell you through my lens: Whether beautiful or ugly, all that happens on this land is reminding us to love and cherish the land beneath our feet.

Chi Po-lin Foundation, Editorial Department excerpt

龜山島日出

Sunrise over Guishan Island

宜蘭　Ilan　2002

宜蘭龜山島是北台灣生態旅遊和觀賞鯨豚的
勝地，「龜山朝日」被列為蘭陽八景之首，
不同的季節與時間有不一樣的景觀變化，魅
力無窮。

Ilan's Guishan Island is a well-known scenic spot for
ecotourism and whale watching in northern Taiwan.
The sunrise over Guishan is regarded as one of the
eight great scenic sights of the Lanyang Plain. Different
seasons and times put their own variations on this
infinitely charming vista.

看見台灣，看見齊柏林

蕭瓊瑞

國立成功大學歷史學系教授

台灣藝術家開始深刻觀察自己的土地，描繪、詮釋自己的土地，是始於日治中期；在石川欽一郎 (1871-1945) 老師的教導下，台灣的年輕人開始學會用自己的眼睛觀看自己的土地、用畫筆描繪自己的土地。從剛直有力的高山稜線、婀娜多姿的相思林木、蓊鬱紛雜的竹林樹叢、低矮溫馨的農村屋舍，到新建龐然的台北鐵橋，和巍峨矗立的總督府……，台灣的藝術家以他們一生的歲月，為台灣留下了歷史的見證，也呈顯了屬於那個時代的心靈絮語。

戰後台灣，由於政治的戒嚴，藝術家對山林、海邊這些屬於「國防重地」的描繪受到限制，轉而以城鎮、鄉野風光為主軸，甚至走向超現實或抽象的創作路向，和土地的直接對話，也相對薄弱；即使鄉土運動時期，藝術家的眼光，仍集中在破敗的農村，以及帶著懷舊感傷的民俗文物。

齊柏林以他特殊的職業關係，有機會為台灣的土地測量、山林紀錄，搭乘直升機，從高空的角度俯瞰台灣的土地，＂Ilha Formosa＂當年西方殖民主義者，乘船途經台灣東部海面，驚見台灣山林的美麗，不禁讚歎：美麗之島；現在齊柏林再度帶領人們，拉高視角，俯看這個山脈連綿、溪流蜿蜒、田野翠綠的美麗之島。

台灣，一個地球生態上的奇景，在最大的海洋板塊（太平洋板塊）和最大的陸地板塊（歐亞陸塊）巨大推擠下，遠在 2000 多萬年前，也就是喜馬拉雅造山運動時，便浮出了海洋的表面；之後再經菲律賓板塊的插入擠壓，形成了今天的樣貌。在東西不到 140 公里的寬度上，超過 3000 公尺以上的高山，竟然超過 200 多座。這些高山，站立在亞熱帶的緯度上，山頂卻是酷冷的寒帶；多樣性的氣溫變化，孕育了豐富的林相，也造就了全世界最豐富的生態變化。從原生種、特有種，到變異種，台灣的生態樣貌，是自然界的奇觀；以蝴蝶為例，整個歐洲計有 200 多種，一個小小的台灣，卻擁有 400 多種。

齊柏林自空中俯視的台灣，是如此的美麗。他不再是一個單純的記錄者，而是一個「美」的發現者、詮釋者，乃至守護者，最後變成一個藝術家；為了拍攝更理想的畫面，他在幾無奧援的情形下，不斷地增添設備，提升品質。一次又一次地拍攝，累積了大量的底片，有些是交給業務單位的結業報告，但更多的是心血的結晶，也是創作的成果。

在長年的拍攝中，齊柏林看見了台灣的美，也看見了土地的被破壞；而那樣快速地破壞，讓他驚心，更讓他憂慮。從礦坑的挖掘、山坡地的濫墾、濫建，乃至海岸的開發，他提醒政府，

Seeing Taiwan, Seeing Chi Po-lin

Hsiao Chong-ray

Taiwan artists began to pay close attention to and interpret their own land visually during the middle period of Japanese rule. Under the guidance of the teacher Ishikawa Kin'ichiro (1871-1945), young artists in Taiwan learned to observe their land with their own eyes and then paint from their observations. From straight and powerful mountain ridgelines, graceful Taiwan acacia forests, dense bamboo groves, and cozy farmhouses, to majestic Taipei bridge and imposing Governor-General's Office (today's Presidential Office Building), Taiwan's artists took to spending their lives bearing witness both to history and to the zeitgeist of their eras.

Professor of History,

National Cheng Kung University

During the martial law era after World War II, artists were restricted in how they could depict forests and beaches due to "national defense" considerations, so they turned to urban and agrarian landscapes instead. Some even worked in the genres of surrealism or abstract expressionism. Consequently, their direct dialogues with the land were not as robust as in earlier eras. Even during the nativist movement, artists tended to focus on run-down farming villages and folk artifacts that evoked a sense of nostalgia.

Because of his unusual profession, Chi Po-lin had opportunities to survey the land and record the forests of Taiwan from the high vantage point of a helicopter. The Portuguese, who would eventually colonize the island, were stunned by Taiwan's beauty as they sailed past eastern Taiwan. They called it "Ilha Formosa," which means "beautiful island." Today, Chi Po-lin's photography once again takes us airborne to look at the expansive mountains, winding rivers and green fields of this beautiful island.

Taiwan is one of the earth's ecological marvels. Over 20 million years ago, when the Himalayan Mountains were being formed, the island of Taiwan was pushed out of water by a collision of the largest ocean plate (the Pacific Plate) with the largest land plate (the Eurasian Plate). Later, as a portion of the Eurasian Plate became subducted beneath remnants of the Philippine Sea Plate, Taiwan geologically became what it is today. On an island less than 140 kilometers wide, there are remarkably over 200 mountains with elevations of at least 3,000 meters. Although located in the subtropics, these mountains' upper slopes are very cold. The varied climatic zones nurture many kinds of forests and ecosystems, which are among the world's most diverse. In terms of the number of native species, endemic species, and variant species, Taiwan's natural environment is a marvel. Take, for instance, butterflies. In all of Europe, there are only 200-some-odd species of butterfly, but there are more than 400 in the much smaller area of Taiwan.

Chi Po-lin's Taiwan, which is seen from above, is breathtakingly beautiful. Not merely a photographer leaving a record, he became someone who discovered, interpreted, and even guarded beauty. Ultimately, he became an artist. To capture the best shots, he continued to add to his equipment in order to raise the quality of his work, but he did so virtually without any outside support. He accumulated a huge number of negatives. Some of these he shot for his government work, but he retained many more as the fruits of his creativity or as the personal crystallizations of his blood, sweat, and tears.

Over the years, Chi Po-lin saw both the beauty of Taiwan as well as the ugliness of a land being bruised and battered. The speed of destruction scared and worried him. Witnessing the overdevelopment of coasts and the mining, deforestation and overdevelopment of mountain slopes, he reminded Taiwan's

更提醒人民：台灣必須被認識，更必須被保護，於是有了《看見台灣》的發行。

齊柏林猶如《舊約聖經》中那些呼籲災難即將來臨的先知，疾呼吶喊，聲嘶力竭；人們在觀賞《看見台灣》影片時，有驚豔，也有心痛，然而救急圖存的腳步始終蹣跚。

日本知名小說家三島由紀夫，以一次金閣寺火災的新聞為靈感，假想那是一位視金閣寺為至美象徵的小和尚，為了極力保護她而不能，終於放火燒了她，也因此創生了永世的文學經典。

齊柏林愛台灣、不忍台灣被傷害，最後以自身為祭品，殉身於拍攝的過程中；他以生命成全了台灣這個美麗之島的發現與存續。

齊柏林讓人們看見台灣，人們卻忘記或至少是忽略了齊柏林自己；他不只是一個單純的影像記錄者，更是一位帶著理想與美的追求的傑出藝術家。

齊柏林為了拍攝的理想，毅然辭去穩定的工作；為了畫面的品質，在好友的支持下，湊足金額前往美國購買一台專門高空拍攝的陀螺儀；未料，帶著機器準備返台時，才發現忘了估算運輸及關稅的費用。最後，齊柏林竟然將機器拆解成數大箱，以隨身行李的方式，一人扛回台灣。

齊柏林是完美主義者，所有拍攝的影片或照片，都是一再地計劃、一再地調整、一再地篩選。在《看見台灣》的影片中，我們隨著齊柏林的眼睛、速度，平緩而深情地見到台灣的美麗與哀愁；他也藉此激起了台灣國土保護、生態護育的行動。

收錄在《凝視 齊柏林》書中的，則完全是呈顯台灣山岳、海岸、田野、溪流……之美：那位在北緯 23°28' 14"、東經 120°56' 56" 的玉山主峰，作為台灣百岳龍頭，昂然偉立，掩映在山嵐雲海之中；連綿的龍脈，向有「台灣屋脊」的美稱，護障著台灣的生態、居民。台灣山嶽之美，時而如碎石坡那樣的一瀉千里，令人驚心；時而如九九峰的群峰聳立、連綿不絕。在自然之美外，齊柏林的鏡頭也捕捉了人文之美，那是人們為了生活，在美麗的大地上刻劃下的圖案，從那幅知名的稻田上的大腳印，到雲林口湖鄉的魚塭、蚵田、台南青鯤鯓的扇形鹽田、屏東大鵬灣的蚵架，乃至巴士海峽的定置漁網，和漁船尾巴畫出來的白色浪花……。

小小的台灣島，卻擁有全世界最豐富的海岸地形，從岬角、沙岸、斷層，到珊瑚礁、濕地等，豐富的海岸地形，也蘊生了多樣的人文生態。齊柏林的鏡頭，善於截取畫面、掌握光影，搭配藍天、白雲、海洋的襯托，讓造化的美麗，成為畫面的永恆，色彩飽和而層次分明。

齊柏林透過相機，讓人們看見了台灣；人們似乎也應該透過這些台灣之美，重新「看見齊柏林」：一位透過影像，讓人們拉高視角看見自我土地的傑出藝術家，也是為台灣留住美麗的守護天使、上帝的代言人。

government and people that the island needed to be understood and protected. It was in that spirit that he directed *Beyond Beauty—Taiwan from Above*.

Like the prophets in the Old Testament who foresaw the coming of calamities, Chi Po-lin called people's attention to the potential of future devastation. When people watch his film, they are astonished by its beauty but also pained that the steps being taken to save Taiwan from environmental devastation are still so slow.

Mishima Yukio, a famous Japanese novelist, based his masterpiece *The Temple of the Golden Pavilion* on news about a fire at the pavilion. He imagined a young monk who saw the Golden Pavilion as the symbol of ultimate beauty. Because he could not protect her, in the end he put fire to her.

Chi Po-lin loved Taiwan, and he couldn't bear to see it harmed. In the end, he sacrificed himself to the filming of his beloved. He used his life to facilitate the discovery and continued existence of this beautiful island.

Chi Po-lin led people to see Taiwan, but people forget or ignored Chi himself. He was not merely a photographer; he was also an outstanding artist who pursued beauty and his ideals.

To pursue his mission of filming Taiwan, Chi Po-lin left a job with a stable income. To improve the quality of his shots, he, with friends' help, raised the money to purchase a special camera stabilizer for aerial photography in the United States. When he was about to come back to Taiwan, he realized that he had forgotten to calculate the shipping and customs fees. In the end, he dismantled the machine and packed the parts into several suitcases, bringing it back all by himself.

Chi Po-lin was a perfectionist. He planned, adjusted, and repeatedly sorted through all the footage and photographs he took. In Beyond Beauty—Taiwan from Above, we follow his eyes and pacing to see the beauty and sadness of Taiwan. In turn, Chi leveraged the film's success to initiate a movement to protect Taiwan's natural environment.

Photographs in this book convey the beauty of Taiwan's mountains, coasts, fields, and rivers in their full glory. The main peak of Mount Jade (with the coordinates of 23°28' 14" N and 120°56' 56" E), is the highest mountain in Taiwan. It stands majestically lofty, shrouded in mountain mists and a sea of clouds. Its extended ridgeline, which is known as the roof of Taiwan, protects the ecology and residents of Taiwan. The beauty of Taiwan's mountains sometimes manifests as frightening scree and sometimes as the unending 99 Peaks. Besides images of nature, Chi Po-lin's camera also captured the beauty of Taiwan's culture. There are images of marks that people have left on the land in pursuit of making a living— from the famous big foot print on a rice paddy, the fish ponds and oyster farms of Hukou Township in Yunlin County, the fan-shaped salt fields in Qingkunshen of Tainan, and the oyster racks in Dapeng Bay of Pingtung, to the stationary fishing nets in the Bashi Channel and the white wakes of fishing boats….

Taiwan, though tiny, has some of the richest costal landforms in the world—from capes, sandy coasts and fault coasts, to coral reefs and wetlands. These rich coastal landforms have given birth to diverse humanistic ecologies. Chi Po-lin was good at capturing images and controlling the lighting, and at using the sky, the clouds and the ocean as foils. His photos have saturated colors and distinct layers, and he brought eternity to these images of natural beauty.

Through his camera, Chi Po-lin let people see Taiwan. It seems that in turn people should, through these beautiful images of the island, rediscover Chi himself—an outstanding artist who elevated people to gain perspective on their own land, as well as a guardian angel and a spokesman for God about Taiwan's beauty.

一位理性與情感兼俱的空中攝影家

林志明

國立台灣美術館 館長

影像藝術家齊柏林以 2013 年發表的代表作《看見台灣》聞名於世，後來不幸地因為拍攝續集《看見台灣 II》在 2017 年墜機去世。雖然大多數的人是因為這部意義深遠，和前後許多攝影及影像作品一起喚醒台灣人民環保意識的空拍紀錄片而認識齊柏林，不過他所常期耕耘的，卻是攝影中特別的一個支脈，一般稱為航空攝影或空中攝影（Aerial photography or airborne imagery）。

在航空攝影這個領域，齊柏林是台灣的翹楚之一，他累積的飛行時數達到 2500 小時以上，拍攝影像超過 30 萬幅。然而由於拍攝必須租用直昇機，再加上購買昂貴的專業設備，齊柏林的投入可以用傾家盪產加以描述。而且他對航空攝影的熱愛，也幾近可以用瘋狂兩字來形容。就像他的名字，雖然是本名，但和歷史上著名的德國飛船發音相似，仿佛是一種宿命的印記。

回顧空中攝影的歷史，最早可以回溯到 1858 年法國攝影師 Nadar（Gaspard-Félix Tournachon）：他搭乘熱氣球升空，在巴黎上空拍攝了第一張空中攝影照片。由於早期攝影的工作程序相對複雜，必須在熱氣球的籃室中建立完整的工作設備（想像一座小型化學實驗室），Nadar 花費多年的時間才獲得成功，可惜的是他所攝照片並沒有被保留下來。現今留下的是當年描畫這個事件的幾張諷刺漫畫，見證其轟動程度。其中有一張描繪 Nadar 在熱氣球上拍攝巴黎，下面景像中的樓房上都寫著斗大的法文 photographie（攝影），顯示出一種上下交織的狂熱狀態。諷刺漫畫的圖說是「Nadar 將攝影提昇到藝術的境界」，巧妙地將攝影升空與人們當對攝影普遍的質疑連結在一起。

快速地翻閱空中攝影史，可以看到一種類似狂熱的驅動力，除了熱氣球，在飛機發明之前，風箏、鴿子或是火箭也都是受到空中攝影眷顧的載體。使用風箏拍攝，除了載重的問題之外，還需處理自動快門的驅動方式。使用鴿子作載體，則需發明將整個攝影設備微形化的裝置；火箭則明顯具有回收底片的問題待解決。1897 年，著名的諾貝爾獎創立人瑞典籍 Alfred Nobel 本人就是第一位成功使用火箭拍攝照片的發明家。飛機、直升機等現代航空器發明之後，因為便利性和可操作性大增，取代了先前的各種模式。當代的航空攝影要面對的根本問題則是，當功能強大的無人機及機上微型攝影設備發明之後，攝影師是否仍要冒險升空，親自拍攝？

An Aerial Photographer both Rational and Sensitive

Lin Chi-ming

Director of the National Taiwan
Museum of Fine Arts

The photographic artist Chi Po-lin became renowned for his 2013 film Taiwan from Above. Later, he had the misfortune of dying while filming the sequel to that film in 2017. Although most people became acquainted with Chi through his documentary, which awakened a sense of environmental consciousness in Taiwan, Chi himself had long worked in the specialized field of aerial photography (or airborne imagery).

Chi was one of Taiwan's leading aerial photographers, accumulating more than 2500 hours in the air and more than 300,000 aerial photographs. Yet because one must rent a helicopter for aerial photography and purchase expensive specialized equipment, Chi Po-lin can be fairly described as nearly bankrupting himself in the process. Meanwhile, his passion for aerial photography can be fairly described as fanatic and even perhaps borne out by his name. Although Chi Po-lin was the name given to him at birth, it sounds very close to the Chinese word for Zeppelin. Thus, it almost seems as if he were fated to pursue his calling.

The history of aerial photography dates as far back as 1858, to the French photographer Gaspard-Félix Tournachon, who was known as Nadar. Nadar flew over Paris in a hot-air balloon, taking the first aerial photographs. Because early photographic processes were complicated, it was necessary to set up a complete workroom (think small chemistry lab) in the balloon's basket. Nadar spent many years in pursuit of aerial shots before finally succeeding. Unfortunately, none of his photographs have survived. What have survived are several contemporaneous cartoons making fun of his efforts. These cartoons document what a sensation he was causing. One cartoon shows Nadar in a hot air balloon photographing Paris. At the bottom of the image, the word "photographie" (photography) is written on every building. The whole composition demonstrates a sense of the craze surrounding photography at the time. The caption reads, "Nadar raises photography to the realm of art." It marvelously connects the idea of aerial photography to the general doubts that people had about photography at the time.

A quick glance at the history of aerial photography provides a look at the fa natical driving force behind this art form. In addition to hot air balloons, there were kites, pigeons and rockets used for aerial photography before the invention of airplanes. Kites struggled bearing loads of much weight and required inventing an automatic way to snap the shutter. The use of pigeons, meanwhile, necessitated the invention of miniaturized photo equipment. The use of rockets posed problems with retrieving the negatives. In 1897 Alfred Nobel, the Swedish founder of the Nobel prize, was the first person to successfully use a rocket for photography. When modern aircraft, such as airplanes and helicopters, came into existence, they replaced all the previous means of aerial photography thanks to their increased convenience and operability. Today the fundamental question faced by aerial photographers is this one: With the advent of drones and micro cameras, why should aerial photographers risk going airborne themselves?

這個問題，可惜已來不及提問齊柏林本人，不過由他結束生命的方式是搭乘直升機拍攝遇險來看，我猜測他會是堅持要冒險升空的一位。這個堅持或許可以使我們觀看他的攝影作品時，有另一層體悟。

法國哲學家 - 社會學家 Michel de Certeau 曾把由高空觀看城市和在地上行走城市加以對比，指出前者是一種理性的觀點，可以笛卡爾式地看到都市的佈局、組織和結構；後者則是身體力行且充滿衝突和意外，卻是人們每日以腳書寫的詩句。升空拍攝地景，也同樣是一種視角的轉換。早在前述的 Nadar 之前，印象派時期的畫家 Gustave Caillebotte 就曾試驗俯視的視角，而後來蘇聯時期的 Alexander Rodchenko 更是拍出了具有強烈視覺衝擊性的俯視影像，成為 1920 年代新視象運動中的代表性人物。

和這些攝影史上著名的人物相對比，齊柏林有數個特點會突顯出來。首先他拍攝的對象雖然是自然和人文景象兼俱的，但在自然之中會看到許多紋理、樣式（pattern），尤其當他後來投入環境保護運動，揭露了許多污染的實況之時，更是如此。由這一點來看，齊柏林雖然也拍攝出許多壯麗台灣風景，但我認為他更是一位企圖傳遞訊息更勝於造就美麗形式的藝術家。

齊柏林一生接近狂熱地實踐空中攝影，而且親自升空直到以身相殉，除了空中攝影可以提供的觀察距離之外，相信還有一份強大熱情支持著他。他偏愛使用直升機，可以更自由地飛行，環繞同一對象進行多角度的拍攝。雖然拉開距離的視角，天然地具有一種理性的態度，但因為他的環繞拍攝，也是一種花費時間和心力的工作方式，他那彷彿是在梳理著台灣土地及水文各種面貌的手勢，也使他的作品富含著感情的成份。

Unfortunately, it's too late to ask this question to Chi Po-lin himself. But since his life ended on a helicopter in pursuit of aerial photography, I can guess that he was determined to take that risk. Understanding that determination may provide us with another level of understanding his work.

Michel de Certeau, a French philosopher and social scientist, once compared looking at a city from the air versus looking at it from street level. He pointed out that the former took a rational perspective, offering a Cartesian look at the city's layout, organization and structure. The latter, on the other hand, is a lived perspective, full of conflicts and accidents, as well as the poetry of life written every day by people's own feet. Aerial photography, meanwhile, is a kind of transformation of perspective. Long before the aforementioned Nadar, the impressionist painter Gustave Caillebotte once experimented with bird's eye views, and later the Soviet artist and photographer Alexander Rodchenko would shoot some bird's eye photography that had a strong visual impact. He would become a representative figure of the 1920s "New Vision Photography" movement.

In comparison to many of these famous figures in the history of photography, Chi po-lin has several special characteristics. First, although both natural and human landscapes were the subject of his photography, in nature one can see many textures and patterns. In particular, after he threw himself into the environmental movement, he exposed many incidents of pollution, where these patterns and textures were even more obvious. Hence, although Chi Po-lin has photographed much magnificent scenery in Taiwan, I believe that he is an artist more concerned with conveying a message than with creating or conveying beautiful forms.

Chi Po-lin spent his life in the fanatic pursuit of aerial photography, continually flying to get shots until he gave up his life. Aerial photography provided the perspective of distance, but there was more to it than that: A strong passion was supporting his quest. He loved the greater freedom he got flying in helicopters, freedom that allowed him to circle his subjects and find different angles to shoot. Although pulling back for greater perspective naturally leads to a more rational attitude, his time-consuming and psychologically taxing method of circling for shots led him to comb through the landscapes and waterscapes of Taiwan. It led to richness and detail that have invested his works with great sensibility.

昨日仍然美麗與驚歎

劉克襄

作家

空拍，或者說空中攝影所展現的作品，一定有某種致命吸引力，在平常難以想像的高度裡，讓人從天上往下俯瞰時，激發了大家內心深處的共鳴。

最普遍的經驗便是搭飛機。當你即將降落，如果坐的位置在窗口，天氣晴朗，高度又適當。值此一刻，往下凝視，往往會看到動人的奇妙景觀。山野是那麼深邃地壯闊開展，綺麗色塊的土地也恢宏地綿綿迤邐。

縱使那是一處熟悉的地方，都能出奇地像魔術裡變化出來的萬千織錦。因為在空中，在飛鳶盤旋的位置，你有了嶄新的體驗。此時，手邊如果有攝影器材，你不免想取出，記錄這一罕見的綺麗畫面，深怕以後就再也沒有緣分。

而你確實就常這麼擁有一、二次機會，積極地按下快門。只可惜，我們不是專業人士，難以理想取鏡。但縱使你是攝影專家，有機會飛上高空，也不見得能拍出期待的構圖。

美景雖在，空拍卻非一蹴可幾。即使再好的角度和天氣，都不是一次或三、四次的飛行，便可臻及的藝術殿堂。除了特殊器材的配備，空中攝影的專業和艱苦，以及事前的準備，都遠遠超乎尋常的想像。

你必須擁有異於常人的狂熱，兩、三百次以上巡航的歷練，才可能實踐。每一次出發都是飛行的探險，連續下來才可能創造史詩般的壯遊。截至目前，全台也只有齊柏林願意付出，完整地燃燒熱情，實踐此一空前的盛事。

初次看到齊柏林的照片是透過月曆。翻完連續十二張，不用文字旁白，就被攝影裡面的畫面構圖震懾。月曆的空拍當然是精挑細選。一張張動人的圖片後面，隱藏了諸多繁複的因素。合宜的日子，允當的路線，適當的季節，以及豐富的閱景經驗，幾乎缺一不可，也幾無幸運可言。

飛行攝影也跟登高山一樣，需要龐大資金和器材設備的奧援。但空中攝影師非登山家，來到一個岔路，可以好整以暇地找出地圖和指北針，仔細揣摩和研究。飛行攝影可不容許蹉跎，在經費考量下，飛到地點時，你必須確切定位，清楚掌握當下，知道要拍攝哪些物件，以及發現新的可能。

飛行之前，你早就大量閱讀，熟悉地理山川，作為判斷的依據，並且準備好各種因應的計劃。透過多方知識的養成，經過反覆的抵臨現場，你沉思的也不只是熟悉的地景，而是面

Yesterday, Marvelous and Beautiful

Liu Ke-xiang

Aerial photography, or should I say works of aerial photography, possess a certain fatal attraction. Taken at normally unimaginable heights, these works looking down from the air call to something deep within people.

The most common experience people have with these vantage points are on airplanes. If you are sitting in a window seat and there is no cloud cover when a plane descends, you may find yourself at exactly the right altitude to see amazing vistas below. The magnificent beauty of the mountain wildernesses becomes apparent as different patches of color are revealed one after another.

Writer

Even places with which one is familiar can be newly revealed as marvelously variegated tapestries. That's because when you are in the air in view of soaring eagles, you may experience something entirely new. At this moment, if you have a camera at hand, then you will likely want to pull it out and record that beautiful and rarely glimpsed scene out of fear that you will never be fated to have such an opportunity again.

When granted these opportunities, you frantically click the shutter. But too bad we aren't professionals, and too bad it's so hard to get high-quality shots. And even if you were a professional photographer who had an opportunity to take aerial shots, it's not certain you would get the images you wanted.

In fact, although landscapes from the air are beautiful, aerial photography isn't something that can be mastered quickly Even with good vantage points and weather, there's no guarantee that you will capture exhibition-quality shots on one flight, or even on three or four. In addition to needing special camera equipment and expertise, the preparations required and the hardships encountered in aerial photography far exceed what one might imagine.

You must possess an unusual fanaticism, a history of perhaps 200-300 times in the air before you can take photographs of the highest quality. Each flight is an adventure, but epic results demand repeated efforts. To the present day in Taiwan, only Chi Po-lin has been willing to put forth the required work. Only he possessed the passion to achieve what had been unprecedented in the field.

The first photographs of Chi's that I saw were in a calendar. It is no surprise that outstanding works had been selected. After successively flipping through the 12 images, which lacked captions, I was shocked by the beauty of their compositions. There were many unseen factors behind their excellence, including the choice of suitable seasons, days with good weather, and appropriate routes, as well as Chi's abundant experience in observing landscapes. If any one of these conditions had been missing, then these works never would have come into being. Luck had nothing to do with it.

Aerial photography is like mountaineering: It requires adequate funds and proper equipment. But aerial photographers lack some of the advantages of mountain climbers, who can calmly consult their map and compass when they come to a fork in a trail, carefully considering the best course of action. Aerial photographers cannot squander their time. Out of financial considerations, they must seize the moment and immediately determine the best position to take upon reaching their destinations, knowing what they want to photograph and being open to discovering new possibilities.

Before flying, they must conduct research, gaining knowledge about the lay of the land upon which they can base their decisions and plan for different potential eventualities. With extensive knowledge and repeated experience of the site, they gain, more than mere familiarity, an ability to

對現場狀況，找到一個適合的切入點。

每一張的完成，都是在這樣周延的準備下，完成如詩如畫的構圖。拍攝者透過對這些地理風物的熟悉，找到合宜的高度。一如不同陶瓷的燒冶，必須算準火候。一如蔬果包裝，不能只是亮麗的外表，裡面必須流露呈現栽種過程的用心和栽種的信念。

柏林的作品便是。總能夠說出一些，或者意欲表達什麼。悄然地，孕育一種濃郁的幽微。那樣的內涵，容我爬梳，在前頭冠上一個名詞，人文。而非只是美麗的，缺少溫度的，豐富地景的調和。這些照片展現的，正是一個空中攝影師對這塊土地的熟悉，甚而流露出跟它熱絡對話的親密。這種充滿生態關懷的氣度，並非每一個攝影家都有。

平常跟柏林談台灣各地的地理風貌，他也是少數能提出環境數據論述，跟關心環境者對話的人。很多攝影者只會拍攝，丟出拍好的照片，告訴你拍攝地點，當日天氣，接著告訴你這個地方的位置、地名，或者談出 Google、維基百科應有的資料訊息。

但他不是，隨便調出一張片子，我們總能聊出許多話題。以前他還常看我的臉書，不斷附和，或回應我的論述和觀點。

譬如有一回，我發文感慨，關渡自然公園和基隆河河口中間的產業道路，太過於寬闊。河堤自行車步道又跟著一起並行，從高空觀看一定像把剃刀，把河床的紅樹林、蘆葦叢跟自然公園沼澤區劃分為兩半。溼地經此切割，既缺乏完整性，更嚴重影響水鳥的棲息。沒一個下午，柏林寄來一張關渡空拍圖回應，清楚地把我文章的訴求展示得更加清楚。

還有 2015 年 8 月，蘇迪勒颱風襲台，南勢溪水流暴漲，幾乎淹沒烏來街區。我敘述自己在北勢溪的旅行，看到河上游茶園拓墾的憂心狀態，不禁慶幸雨水滂沱的位置偏南。若是集中在北勢溪，後果會不堪設想。隔日，他馬上提供了周遭的照片作為佐證的對照。

他不只忙碌於空拍，平時即持續關心環境，以專業提供意見，隨時協助有志一同的夥伴。每次拜託需求的空照圖，他也樂於義務提供。有時我會暗自驚訝，想要什麼樣的台灣，哪一個角落的空拍，他好像一個大圖庫，備便在那兒隨時供應我們。

90 年代以來，台灣是何種地景，齊柏林長期默默地從空中觀測，以一己之力，完成一座島兩個年代的紀錄。這一不可能的任務，我還未聽聞其他國家空拍攝影師有此跟時間賽跑的瘋狂壯舉，這也是他長時在空拍裡，留給台灣的最大資產，最美的福報。

如今，這個福報又有了結晶。基金會特別從三十幾萬張照片精挑細選，以此集結成冊。我想這本書背後應當如是理解。讓我們再度跟他回到空中，再次俯瞰大地，以不久前才過去的環境和時日變遷，做為明天的石蕊試紙，繼續看護我們的家園。

adjust to the current situation and to find suitable approaches.

These rigorous preparations are necessary to achieve compositions in photographs comparable to those in poems or paintings. With a geographic familiarity, photographers can find exactly the perfect altitude for individual photographs just as potters use different temperatures to fire different ceramics. Or it's like how fruits and vegetables can't merely be packaged to look good on the outside; what is inside must likewise show that the fruits were planted with care.

This is the case for Chi Po-lin's works: They always are saying or wanting to express something profound and mysterious. Let me give it a name: humanity. And they are not outwardly beautiful photographs that are inwardly lacking in warmth. Rather, these aerial photographs demonstrate their maker's familiarity with the land and even reveal an intimacy that arises from passionate dialog. Their sense of concern for the environment is not something that every photographer can capture.

I used to speak to Po-lin about the appearance of various locales in Taiwan, and he was one of the few photographers concerned with the environment who could cite numbers in his discussions. Many photographers just take pictures and drop off the photos they've taken, going no farther than noting the general area where they were shot and what the weather was like that day. At most they might follow up with the name of the specific location and provide a bit of information they have gleaned from Google or Wikipedia.

But Chi wasn't like that. Randomly picking out one of his photos, we could find all manner of topics to expound upon. He would often look at my Facebook page, liking what I had written or giving me feedback about his own point of view.

Once, for instance, I made a comment lamenting that an industrial road between the Guandu Nature Park and the mouth of the Keelung River was too wide. When added to the bicycle and walking path on the levy, it looked most definitely from the air as if a razor had cut in half the area's natural wetlands (the nature park's swamps and the expanses of mangroves and reeds along the river). With these wetlands carved up, there was a lack of ecological integrity, and it affected the water bird habitat. Later that afternoon, Po-lin sent over a photograph that clearly showed the point I was trying to make.

In August of 2015, Typhoon Soudelor battered Taiwan, and the Nansh River overflowed its banks, flooding much of Wulai. I described my own travels on the Beish River and my fears about how the tea plantations been dangerously expanded there along the upper stretches of the river. I was relieved that the worst of the rain had fallen farther south. If the rainfall had been centered on the Beish River, the result would have been catastrophic. The next day, he immediately provided corroborating photographs for reference and comparison.

He was not just busy with his aerial photography: He regularly showed concern about the environment, providing expert opinions and making himself available to help like-minded people. Whenever anyone asked him for a needed aerial photograph, he would happily oblige. At times I was amazed at how he always seemed able to provide these photographs, regardless of the location or angle requested.

In the 1990s Chi Po-lin began an effort to make long-term observations of Taiwan's landscapes from the air. Thanks to his efforts, we have a record of how landscapes looked in two different eras. It was a mission impossible, a crazy race against time never undertaken by photographers of other nations as far as I know. This is the greatest asset and the most beautiful blessing left by his many years of work as an aerial photographer in Taiwan.

Today this blessing has borne fruit: The Chi Po-lin Foundation has specially selected photos for this book from the more than 300,000 photographs in his personal archive. I think that this is the best way of understanding this book. Let us return to the air and to surveying this vast land, so that these images of changing landscapes will serve as litmus tests that will help us to better care for our land.

我們不會再有第二個齊柏林

陳 文 茜

中天新聞台《文茜的世界周報》主持人

我真正認識齊柏林是因為「八八風災」，讓我看到有一個人，他是真正關心台灣土地的人，而不是關心權力的人，我們因此成為朋友。

我看到他為了籌款拍攝《看見台灣》紀錄片，抵押了自己唯一的房子，他的決心如此強大到這個地步，我心想，如果同樣身為台灣一份子的我們，讓他自己一個人很孤單地去完成他一個人的使命，而他所要完成的，卻是我們所有人都需要的答案跟需要的影片，我覺得台灣這個社會太無情了。

所以我就希望能夠幫他忙，後來《看見台灣》拍攝成功了！但上映之前我很緊張，尤其知道他竟走商業院線，我問柏林：「你為什麼要走商業院線，你難道不知道你會被抽走大多數的錢都到片商那裡去嗎？那麼多人支持你的理由，不是要讓這些人賺錢，是希望你可以持續地工作。」

我教訓了他一頓。聽說那天他回去之後，非常沮喪。他害怕說：「這個原來很支持他的大姐姐，怎麼突然批評他？」我知道這件事，頗不好意思。

不久之後，柏林給我寫了一封信，他就提到當時我的那一番既警示又嚴厲的話語，提醒他不可以把影片「丟」給院線，於是他就開始在每一次電影播放之後，就坐在戲院跟觀眾交流，因為他拍攝電影的目的，是為了要做公民的教育。

當時影片的知名度打開了，各個片商在搶電影播映權的時候，他談的條件就是「我要辦座談會」。那時我就覺得柏林真的是一位非常特別的人。

「看見‧齊柏林基金會」萬冠麗執行長曾經告訴我一個故事：有一次她坐在齊柏林的車上，她說他開車好慢，因為和他人相約，時間快來不及了，她說：「柏林，你可不可以車開快一點點？」齊柏林回說：「萬姐，我必須安全開車，我們一家六口都靠我一個人吃飯。」

他在馬路上開車這麼在乎安全，他上飛機卻不用在乎安全嗎？如果他在乎，就用無人機拍攝即可，為什麼要親自飛上天呢？只為了給我們多一點感情？要賺取我們的眼淚嗎？賺取我們的票房嗎？我想不是的。他想讓我們真正的徹悟，我們是地球公民，是大海的一部分，而為了這樣的一個理念，他又開始了《看見台灣 II》的開鏡。

然而，才進行第一次的「演出」，他上了高空，卻墜落下來了。

有些故事好像必須用悲劇結束。他是一個在高空飛翔的人，不只是拍攝電影，包括他的眼光，包括他的理想，包括他的高度，我們可能不會再有第二個齊柏林，我們永久失去了他，但是我們不要忘記他曾經給我們的典範。

本文整理自《國家地理》雜誌（*National Geographic Magazine*）特刊，2018 年 6 月影音受訪內容

There Will Be No Second Chi Po-lin

Sisy Chen

Host of Sisy's World News

I came to truly know Chi Po-lin because of the flooding associated with Typhoon Morakot. That event showed me that he was someone who cared about the land of Taiwan rather than merely about personal gain. Consequently, we became friends.

I observed that he had mortgaged his only house to fund the documentary *Beyond Beauty—Taiwan from Above*. The extreme length to which he was willing to go was a testament to the strength of his determination. I thought that if his fellow citizens allowed him to complete his mission alone when the answers he was seeking and the film he was making were needed by all of us, then the society of Taiwan would have proven to be heartless.

Hence, I wanted to help him, and later he would indeed successfully finish filming Taiwan from Above. Yet before the film came out, I grew nervous, surprised that he had decided upon a commercial release in theaters. "Why have you opted for a commercial release?" I asked him. "Don't you know that most of the money will be taken by the film distributor? People don't support you so film distributors can make a lot of money; they support you so that you can continue to work."

I thus scolded him. I heard that when he left, he was quite upset. Taken aback, he had asked, "Why did that woman who had been so supportive suddenly criticize me?" When I heard about this, I became quite embarrassed.

Not long after, Po-lin wrote me a letter in which he recalled my harsh words urging him not to "waste" the film on commercial theaters. He explained that in response he was in the theaters after each screening, interacting with the audiences—because his purpose in shooting the film was to educate people.

When the film was gaining buzz and distributors were fighting for the screening rights, he made one condition: "I want to be able to hold seminars at the theaters." At that point I realized that Po-lin was a very special person.

The Chi Po-lin Foundation's executive director Grace Wan has described how she once was late for an appointment when riding in Chi Po-lin's car and criticized his driving. "Po-lin, can you drive a little faster?" she asked. Chi responded, "I must drive safely. My family of six relies on me as the bread winner."

Since he was that concerned about safety when driving, why wasn't he concerned about the inherent risks in flying? Why didn't he shoot with drones instead? Why did he need to go airborne himself? Was it just to give us more expressive shots? Was it to earn our tears or bolster box-office receipts?

I think not. He wanted us to truly recognize that we were citizens of the world. That was what prompted him to start filming *Taiwan from Above II*.

Yet soon after work on the sequel started, he crashed during a flight.

Some stories seemingly must end in tragedy. He was a highflyer, not just in terms of his photography, but also in terms of his vision, his ideals and his character. We may never get a second Chi Po-lin. While we have forever lost him, we don't want to forget the example that he set for us.

This essay is an edited version of one that appeared in the June 2018 traditional Chinese edition of *National Geographic Magazine*.

生命是能夠相互感知的集合體

李家維

國立清華大學生命科學系教授

《科學人》雜誌總編輯

初識齊柏林是在 2004 年，當時我在國立自然科學博物館擔任館長，邀請他來辦一個大型的戶外作品展。從空中看台灣，那些巨大、動人而震撼的圖像，陳設在館前的演化步道，吸引來了無數觀眾。開展時，我們一起漫步其中，聽他詳細地解說。記得我們特別在一幅苗栗山區的鳥瞰圖前駐足許久，圖像中的季節該是五月春初，雪白的油桐花和金黃的相思樹花，難得地同步綻放，漂亮極了。也許，齊柏林這個人就像是漸漸起暖的五月，試圖透過自己的溫度，喚醒所有美麗的事物。

這個記憶也讓我想起了齊柏林的另一幅彩色山林照。眾所周知，台灣的山林青翠茂盛，但總少了些色彩變化。然而，那幅山林照拍攝的是北插天山的秋季，只看見長在稜線上的台灣山毛櫸，換上了秋裝，一片金黃。

台灣山毛櫸的祖先是在冰河期由中國大陸遷播來台，冰河退卻後，被困鎖在北插天山之巔，長期地孤立演化，成為了台灣獨有的新物種。感嘆的是，隨著現今的全球暖化，它們已退無可退，很可能來不及自己遷播到更高的山區去了，人為的協助繁衍也是必然。對照台灣的歷史，更有相似之感，彷彿我們正處在危急存亡之秋，一種迫切感油然而生。

今天活在地球上的生命，是占所有曾經存活過的生命裡非常小一部分，人類也是如此啊。人生就是有個終點，想用什麼方式過日子，是自己的選項。比如說，氣候變遷、環境汙染，是人類在這個時期最大的生存挑戰，芸芸眾生，也是如此。我們每天都面對著各自的生命困境，並在各種掙扎與選擇中，提供了自己的一份見識與力量。一個人的努力即便對大環境的影響有限，但生命是一個能夠相互感知的集合體，齊柏林的努力，便是最好的證明。而齊柏林的離去，則帶給了世人深沉的省思。

Life Is a Collective Whose Parts Are Capable of Mutual Understanding and Feeling

Li Chia-wei

Professor of Life Science
at National Tsing Hua
University and Editor-in-
chief of *Scientific* American,
Taiwan edition

I first became acquainted with Chi Po-lin in 2004. Back then I was serving as director-general of the National Museum of Natural Science, and I invited him to put on a large outdoor exhibition. Looking at Taiwan from the air, those large, moving and mind-blowing images were displayed in front of the museum along the Evolution of Life Trail, and they attracted countless members of the public. At the opening of the exhibition, we walked up the trail together, and I listened carefully to his explanations. In particular I remember that we stopped for a long time in front of a photograph showing a bird's eye view of a mountainous area of Miaoli County. The season in the photo must have been early Spring, in May. It depicted the rare sight of snow-white tung tree blooms and golden Taiwan acacia blooms flowering together. It was extremely beautiful. Perhaps Chi Po-lin was like a slowly warming May that was planning to use its warmth to gradually awaken all things beautiful.

That memory led me to think of another color photograph that Chi Po-lin had taken of a mountain forest. It is widely known that Taiwan's mountain forests are lush and green but often lack changes of color. However, the mountain scene captured in that photo was of fall on Mt. Beichatian. All that could be seen were Taiwan beeches on a ridgeline, creating an expanse of golden yellow with their fall coats.

The ancestors of the Taiwan beech moved here from mainland China during the Ice Age. After the glaciers retreated, they were left in isolation on the upper slopes of Mt Beichatian to evolve over long periods of time and become a new species that is found only in Taiwan. Regretfully, with global warming, these trees might not have enough time to move even higher by themselves. They may need human help to survive. There are indeed similarities between their history and the history of Taiwan. It seems that we are indeed at a critical, life-or-death moment, when there is a growing sense of urgency.

All the life found on earth today comprises but a tiny portion of the life that has existed over the course of history. And the same holds for people. All lives have an ending point, and one makes one's own choices about how to spend one's days. For instance, climate change and environmental pollution are humanity's greatest challenges in this era, and these challenges are the same for all forms of life. Every day each of us faces our own challenges, and the struggles we face and choices we make give us experience and strength. A single individual's hard work on behalf of the environment can only bring limited effects, but life is a collective whose parts are capable of mutual understanding and feeling. Chi Po-lin's work bears witness to this fact, and his passing offers a chance for deep reflection.

埤塘、雲影

Ponds amid the Clouds

桃園 Taoyuan 2016

桃園台地的河川短促，集水區又小，故早年大量
興建埤塘以利農耕灌溉，全盛時期甚至數量上
萬，蔚為地表殊色，「千塘之鄉」美名也不脛而
走。

On the Taoyuan Tablelands, the rivers are short and
rapid, and the water catchment areas small, so farmers
used to build ponds for irrigation. At one time there
were more than 10,000 of them. They are the source
of Taoyuan's nickname: "the land of ponds."

凝　視

本攝影集命名為「凝視　齊柏林：台灣的四維空間」，除了希望在齊柏林以夢想與勇氣，帶領我們以雲的高度看見台灣的同時，我們也能夠在他如風般離去之後，透過他的眼睛、他的作品，回望並凝視齊柏林，紀念之餘，也給予他一個全新的定位。

從選圖與編排上，我們在進入以「自然、生命、土地、和諧」為主題的空間四維前，先選了一系列以「高山」為主的經典空拍圖，回應著齊柏林的自述：「山像是一切事物的起點，是河川的源頭，孕育各種生物，是我原初夢想的起點，也是我投入空拍領域，一個開始的啟發。」

接著，齊柏林的眼睛，再次帶領我們「飛閱台灣」，從海拔最高的地方漸次降下，並由海轉出，我們將會在垂直而多變的地貌變異中，感受到自然的器度；在理應熟悉不過的土地上，看見人與環境如何互動出各種共存的陌生風景，呈現出生命的廣度；在更聚焦於人文物產的景觀中，領略土地所給予人們的能量與溫度；在時間的軸線上，用影像細數台灣這些年來所發生的重大環境事件。

在每一個相對的至高點上，看見一幅幅人與自然之間，共生依存的圖像。而所有的美麗與殘酷，在同一雙眼睛的凝視下，都將成為對世人的提醒，一句不待言說的懇切忠告。

從齊柏林夢想的起點出發，我們想說的或許不是一個夢想如何實踐的故事，而是希望找到將夢想延續下去的方式；關於齊柏林的定位，也許正如同封面書名下鏤刻的經緯度數字，每個高空攝影師在拍下每一張照片的剎那，都擁有一個獨一無二的定位。

邀請您，在這本攝影集中，也按下自己心中的快門，在廣闊無垠的世界中，找到自己的定位。

執行總監　黃寶琴

This collection of photographs is named *In Focus: Chi Po-lin and Taiwan's Four-Dimensional Spacetime.* The embodiment of Chi's dreams and courage, it offers a view of Taiwan from the vantage point of the clouds. Now that Chi has passed away, it is our hope that these works will allow us to reassess his vision and artistry.

From selecting the photos to laying out the book, we have emphasized four main themes: "nature, life, the land, and harmony." We first selected a series of his classic aerial photos of high mountains that bear witness to his own estimation of those natural features: "Mountains are like the origins of all things. They are the starting points of rivers and support all manner of wildlife. They are where my dreams start, and they are also where I started in aerial photography—the very source of my inspiration."

Then we let Chi's eyes once again lead us to "fly over Taiwan," gradually descending from high elevations before turning at the sea, as we experience a wide variety of landscapes and the majesty of Mother Nature. Although one might think that we citizens of Taiwan should be highly familiar with all these landscapes, Chi shows us how people and the natural environment affect each other and coexist in strange ways, and he captures images of all manner of unfamiliar landscapes that reveal the diversity of life on the island. When photography is more focused on the sites connected to human civilization, it allows us to experience the power and warmth that the land gives people. Plotted on a timeline, these photographs of Chi's can be used to detail major environmental incidents that have befallen Taiwan in recent years.

From high vantage points, we are presented with one image after another of people coexisting with nature. And all the beauty and cruelty that were the focus of one pair of eyes become a reminder to the people of the world, a form of unspoken advice.

We start with the inspiration for Chi Po-lin's dreams, but the story we want to tell may well be more about extending dreams than realizing them. Perhaps, like the latitude and longitude numbers found under the book's title, each moment that an aerial photographer uses to capture an image has its own unique status.

As you peruse this collection of photography, may you find a shutter to click in your own mind and a place for yourself in this vast world.

Executive Director Huang Pao-chin

山像是一切事物的起點，是河川的源頭，孕育各種生物，是我原初夢想的起點，
也是我投入空拍領域，一個開始的啟發。

"Mountains are like the origins of all things. They are the starting points of rivers and support all manner of wildlife.

They are where my dreams start, and they are also where I started in aerial photography—the very source of my inspiration."

齊柏林
Chi Po-lin

前 導　　夢 想 的 起 點

Preface　　The Starting Point of Dreams

玉山主峰、北峰氣象站雪景

Snow at the Yushan Weather Station

南投　Nantou　2005

玉山是台灣第一高峰，北峰峰頂的玉山氣象站標
高 3850 公尺，在東北亞國家中亦無出其右。

Yushan is the highest mountain in Taiwan. The Yushan
Weather Station, located on the summit of its northern
peak at an elevation of 3,850 meters, is the highest
weather station in Northeast Asia.

玉山山脈群峰

Peaks of the Yushan Range

南投　Nantou　年代不詳　Undated

玉山群峰與周邊地域於 1985 年劃定為國家公園，四季景致各具殊色，在布農族與鄒族心目中更是永遠心存敬畏的「聖山」。

Yushan's several peaks and the area around them were designated as a national park in 1985. A sacred mountain revered by the Bunun and Tsou people, Yushan has four distinct seasons, each beautiful in its own way.

玉山主峰
Yushan Main Peak
南投　Nantou　2005

台灣的高山密度驚人，但囿於緯度與氣候，白茫茫的雪景卻非終年可見，只有當強烈大陸冷氣團甚至寒流來襲、水氣豐沛時才有機會出現。

Taiwan has a great number of mountains relative to its area. Yet because it is situated at a subtropical latitude, snow is only possible when there is a strong continental air mass and the humidity is high.

玉山峰起雲湧
The Surging Clouds of Yushan
南投　Nantou　年代不詳　Undated

台灣百岳之首的玉山，由群峰環繞著海拔 3952 公尺的主峰，在雲嵐之中盡顯睥睨天下的磅礴氣勢。

The main peak of Yushan at 3,952 meters above sea level, highest of the "100 Peaks of Taiwan," looks awe-inspiring and majestic amid the clouds.

玉山雪地登山隊

Hikers on Yushan

南投　Nantou　2005

玉山是台灣精神的象徵，許多嚮往山林世界的民眾，都把攀登玉山視為一生當中不容錯過的挑戰。

Yushan is the symbol of the spirit of Taiwan. Many mountain lovers regard climbing Yushan as a challenge that they must tackle at least once in their lifetime.

玉山群峰與南二段
Peaks of Yushan and Southern Section Second Trail
花蓮　Hualien　年代不詳　Undated

中央山脈縱貫南北，向有「台灣屋脊」之稱，其中，
自大水窟迤邐至向陽山的南二段，與玉山「爭鋒」
相對，是登山界著名的縱走路線之一。

The Central Mountain Range, which is called the "roof
of Taiwan," stretches nearly the length of the island
from north to south. The Southern Section Second
Trail, running from Mt. Dashuiku to Mt. Xiangyang and
offering views of Yushan, is a famous hiking route.

雪山主峰雪景

The Snow At Mt. Xue Main Peak

台中　Taichung　年代不詳　Undated

雪山主峰高達 3886 公尺，在日治時期是僅次於玉山的「次高山」，比富士山還要高。山巔被學者發現留有冰河期的「冰斗」地形遺跡，外形呈碗狀的冰斗，也被稱為「圈谷」，是雪山的招牌景致。

At an elevation of 3,886 meters, the main peak of Mt. Xue was known as Tsugitakayama ("second highest peak") during the Japanese occupation, since it is second in Taiwan only to Yushan and is taller than Mount Fuji. Near the peak of Mt. Xue, there is a bowl-shaped glacial cirque that scientists have determined was left from the ice age. It has become one of the features that the mountain is most known for.

穆特勒布山雪景

Snow-Capped Mt. Metelebu

苗栗、台中　Miaoli and Taichung

年代不詳　Undated

雪霸國家公園境內的穆特勒布山，屬於雪山山脈，海拔 3626 公尺，標高在聖稜線上排名第 5，由於山形峻美非凡，山友一致認為是台灣百岳遺珠中的第一順位。

Mt. Metelebu, located in Shei-Pa National Park, is part of the Mt. Xue Range. At an elevation of 3,626 meters, it is the fifth highest peak on the Holy Ridge. Because of its extremely beautiful appearance, many hikers regard its absence from "The Hundred Peaks of Taiwan" as that list's biggest snub.

北一段眺望聖稜線

Looking at the Holy Ridge from
North Section First Trail

宜蘭　Ilan　2010

台灣 3000 公尺以上高峰比比皆是，高來高去，
從中央山脈北一段（南湖大山、中央尖山）望
去，與天邊接壤的正是雪山到大霸尖山的聖稜
線。

Taiwan is home to numerous peaks over 3,000 meters. As one looks out from the Central Mountain Range's North Section First Trail, which runs from Mt. Nanhu to Mt. Zhongyangjian, the horizon is filled by the Holy Ridge, which stretches from Mt. Xue to Mt. Dabajian.

玉山主峰（南北向）

Yushan Main Peak (North-South Orientation)

南投　Nantou　2014

台灣超過 3000 公尺以上的高山多達 268 座，更有匯集奇、險、峻、秀等不同景觀的台灣百岳，玉山作為箇中代表，名實相符。

There are more than 268 mountains over 3,000 meters in Taiwan. Among these, the "100 Peaks of Taiwan" were selected for being especially unique, perilous, steep, or beautiful. Mt. Yu is the most representative of them all.

玉山主峰碎石坡
The Scree of Yushan's Main Peak

南投　Nantou　2014

玉山主峰地形四周各有不同風貌，南北兩側呈千
仞峭壁，西向是高聳深塹，東邊則為碎石陡坡，
其一瀉千里的景象尤其令人驚心動魄。

The terrain of Yushan's main peak differs greatly on each
side. Whereas the south and north sides are steep cliffs,
there is a deep ravine on the west side, and the east side
features scree with scarily loose footing.

大霸尖山

Mt. Dabajian

苗栗 Miaoli 2015

大霸尖山標高 3492 公尺，在台灣百岳中排名 28，與中央尖山、達芬尖山合稱「三尖」，崖壁懸垂陡峭是其最大景觀特色，地質成因為特殊的「箱型褶皺」，附近居民習慣稱之為「酒桶山」。

Mt. Dabajian rises 3,492 meters and ranks 28th among Taiwan's mountains. Along with Mt. Zhongyangjian and Mt. Dafenjian, it is one of the "Three Pointy Peaks." Its imposing "box-fold cliff face" is its most distinctive scenic feature. Locals call it "Wine Cask Mountain."

小觀音山、竹子山
Mt. Xiaoguanyin and Mt. Zhuzi

新北、台北　New Taipei and Taipei　2010

台灣較典型的火山地形主要集中在北部的大屯山火山群，大部分劃歸陽明山國家公園，但見山脈起伏、稜線分明，其中小觀音山一帶則多屬軍事管制區域。

The Tatun Volcanos of northern Taiwan account for most of the island's volcanic landforms. These in turn are mostly located within Yangmingshan National Park, including the area around Mt. Xiaoguanyin, which is largely under military control. These mountains feature clean, distinct ridgelines.

九九峰
99 Peaks

南投　Nantou　2008

九九峰由礫岩層堆疊成群峰聳立的景致，斷崖聳立，並以奇特地景劃為自然保留區。1999 年集集地震後，峰群一夜禿頂，時隔 20 年，終又漸漸回復蒼翠的面貌，鮮活見證了土地與環境的變遷。

Conglomerate rocks layered in groups created the lofty 99 Peaks. The unique topography has made the area worthy of being designated as a nature reserve. After the 921 Earthquake in 1999, the mountains became bare overnight. Twenty years later, they have gradually recovered and turned green again. The changes bear witness to Taiwan's ever-evolving environment.

北插天山

Beichatian Mountain

桃園　Taoyuan　2014

北插天山屬北台灣著名的中級山，享譽之處在
於珍貴的冰河時期子遺物種——台灣山毛櫸，
每屆深秋，豔黃的山頭必定引來無數追焦的登
山客。

Mt. Beichatian is a well-known mid-level mountain in
northern Taiwan that is famous for its stands of Taiwan
beech (*Fagus hayatae*), a species that is a glacial relict.
Every fall, the vibrant yellow leaves of the mountain
attract many hikers.

小尖山、大尖山
Mt. Xiaojian and Mt. Dajian
屏東　Pingtung　2011

山不一定非要比高，尖聳的大尖山終究還是成為
墾丁讓人驚豔的地標，並與小尖山對映成趣，彷
彿電影《魔戒》中的世外桃源場景。

Mountains do not have to be especially tall to be
impressive. Spikey Mt. Dajian, though not particularly tall,
looks spectacular next to Mt. Xiaojian. The vista brings to
mind the otherworldly landscapes in *Lord of the Rings*.

能高安東軍草原
Nenggao-Andongjun Grasslands
花蓮　Hualien　2006

能高山往南至安東軍山這一段稜脊，是中央山脈
縱走的熱門路線之一，綠地毯般的草原景觀迷人，
更有高山湖泊錯落其間，而終年不涸的白石池也
常見水鹿群出沒。

The ridgeline from Mt. Nenggao to Mt. Andongjun is one of the most popular hiking trails of the Central Mountain Range. It passes by charming lush-green grasslands and beautiful alpine lakes. Herds of sambar deer are a common sight by Baishi Pond, which holds water throughout the year.

每條河流都有複雜的支流系統，我常覺得，人生也是如此，由不同的遭遇和經驗組合而成現在這個樣貌。

Every river has a complicated network of tributaries. I often think that people's lives are like that too—

the different encounters and experiences of your past shape what you are today. Standing on the banks of a river upstream,

there's no way to know how the system of tributaries will ultimately shape that river.

齊柏林
Chi Po-lin

自　　然　　的　　器　　度

The Elegance of Nature

大鬼湖

Dagui Lake

台東　Taitung　2005

大鬼湖是魯凱族人的聖湖，過去一度期盼能在此覓得台灣雲豹蹤跡，雖然最後希望落空，仍不稍減此一保育廊道的生態意義與價值。

The Rukai people regard Dagui Lake or "Dalupalringi" (as they call it) a sacred place. At one time, conservationists hoped to find Formosan clouded leopards here. Although that dream was not realized, the reserve still holds important ecological value.

翡翠水庫、北勢溪
Beishi River and Feicui Reservoir

新北　New Taipei　2010

翡翠水庫稱得上是台灣優質水庫的指標，坐落在新店溪支流北勢溪之上，大壩下方並設有一座水力發電站。

The Feicui Reservoir sets the standard for Taiwan's reservoirs. It is located on the Beishi River, a tributary of the Xindian River. There is a hydroelectric plant under the dam.

白石池

Baishi Pond

花蓮　Hualien　2008

能高安東軍草原是中央山脈北三段中的精華，行
經此處的山友必定會造訪海拔超過 3000 公尺的白
石池。山體局部的凹陷，創造了山區生物的重要
水源地，無論是山嵐景色或神出鬼沒的野生動物，
都讓人們一再驚嘆。

The Nenggao-Andongjun Trail is the best section of the Northern Third Section Trail in the Central Mountain Range. No mountaineers who hike this trail would miss Baishi Pond, which is over 3,000 meters above sea level. This small bowl on the mountain serves as an important source of water for wildlife here. The breathtaking scenery, mountain mists, and wildlife charm visitors.

塔瓦溪出海口——沒口溪

The Bar-built Estuary of the Tawa River

屏東　Pingtung　2012

塔瓦溪位於阿朗壹古道北端，蜿蜒河道沒入大海懷
抱的景致震撼人心，幸因旭海—觀音鼻自然保留區
的設立，讓原始礫石海岸的絕美顏色得以維存。

The Tawa River is located on the northern end of
Alangyi Historic Trail. The scenery created by the
winding river flowing into the ocean is magnificent.
Thanks to the establishment of the Xuhai-Guanyinbi
Nature Reserve, the stunning beauty of the unspoiled
gravelly coast has been preserved.

清水斷崖
Qingshui Cliff
花蓮　Hualien　2011

花蓮清水山東側的清水斷崖，一路迤邐蘇花公路和
平至崇德路段，高山雲霧籠罩其間，臨海絕壁千仞
而下，太平洋則海天一色，美如夢幻。

The Qingshui Cliff, on the east side of Qingshui
Mountain in Hualien, runs between Heping and Congde
along the Suao-Hualien Highway. Often shrouded in fog,
the cliff drops straight down into the Pacific. The sight is
simply stunning.

蘭嶼東清
Dongqing Village, Orchid Island

台東　Taitung　2005

位於蘭嶼東北海岸的東清部落，是台灣第一道曙
光照耀的地方，山林與海洋資源極為豐富，誠所
謂：「山是倉庫，海是冰箱。」

Dongqing Village, located on the northeast coast of
Orchid Island, is where the first rays of sun hit Taiwan
every morning. The village sits amid rich mountain
and marine resources. As the local saying goes: The
mountains are the warehouse and the ocean is the
fridge.

立霧溪海岸
Estuary of the Liwu River
花蓮　Hualien　2011

台灣東海岸地質與地形皆具特色，人為干擾也相對較少，以切割出太魯閣峽谷聞名於世的立霧溪，夾帶著大量砂石，於出海之際，在海岸鋪成絕美的弧線。

Relatively undisturbed by people, the east coast of Taiwan features unique geology and terrain. After cutting through Taroko Gorge, the Liwu River flows to the sea carrying large amounts of gravel, which have created a spectacular arc along the coast.

花蓮溪出海口、海岸山脈起點
Hualien River Estuary and
Coastal Mountain Range Origin

花蓮 Hualien 2007

花蓮溪自花東縱谷汨汨北流注入太平洋，出海口沖積造型多變的沙嘴。一旁的花蓮山即海岸山脈北端末梢，海拔 77 公尺，因此又有七七高地之稱。

The Hualien River flows north through the East Rift Valley into the Pacific Ocean. There are many spits in changing shapes near the river mouth. Nearby Hualien Hill represents the northern end of the Coastal Mountain Range. Since it reaches an elevation of 77 meters, it is also known as the "77 Highland."

龜山島

Guishan Island

宜蘭　Yilan　2006

龜山島是一火山島嶼，孤懸於東北角海域，外觀神似海龜擺尾，2000 年以海上生態公園之姿，正式開放限量的登島觀光名額，附近海域亦為鯨豚出沒熱點。

Guishan Island is a turtle-shaped volcanic island that sits by itself in the waters off the northeast coast of Taiwan. In 2000, the island was officially opened to a limited number of visitors. One can often see whales and dolphins in nearby waters.

烏岩角獨木舟

Canoeing in Wuyanjiao

宜蘭　Yilan　2017

烏岩角位於宜蘭南方澳與東澳兩大海灣之間，地形看似並不起眼，卻是中央山脈的起點，更是許多獨木舟玩家嚮往朝聖的秘境。

Wuyanjiao is located in Yilan between the bays of Nanfangao and Dongao. A popular destination for canoe enthusiasts, the location may look insignificant, but it is in fact the starting point of the Central Mountain Range.

蘭嶼划大船獨木舟

Rowing a Large Canoe,
Orchid Island

台東　Taitung　2011

蘭嶼過去因盛產台灣蝴蝶蘭享譽國際蘭花界，而達悟族人的拼板舟也是工藝一絕，憑添「飛魚的故鄉」更多浪漫與傳奇。

Orchid Island's moth orchids have made it world famous among orchid enthusiasts. Likewise, the Tao people's canoes are exceptional works of craftsmanship, which add to the romance and legends associated with the "homeland of the flying fish."

烏石鼻

Wushibi

宜蘭 Yilan 2007

烏石鼻是蘇花海岸中的一條片麻岩脈，比四周更為堅硬，形成了遺世獨立的鼻狀岬角。1994 年時，為了保護海岸環境與原生林，設立了自然保留區，至今仍是一塊人跡罕至的生態寶地。

Located in a remote part of the east coast between Su'ao and Hualien, Wushibi is a nose-shaped cape made of gneiss, which is harder than other rocks in the area. In 1994, in order to protect the coastal environment and the virgin forests here, a nature reserve was established. It is an ecological treasure trove that remains unspoiled today.

野柳岬

Yeliu Cape

新北　New Taipei　2010

遠眺野柳地質公園，貌似海龜俯臥大海一隅，砂岩地質在長年侵蝕及風化的交互作用下，形成各種天然怪石，以女王頭為代表的蕈狀石、燭台石等地形景觀，展現了大自然的鬼斧神工。

From afar, the Yeliu Geopark looks like a sea turtle. Over millennia, the ocean and wind erosion have sculpted the sandstone strata here into oddly shaped rocks. The Queen's Head is the most representative of these masterpieces of Mother Nature.

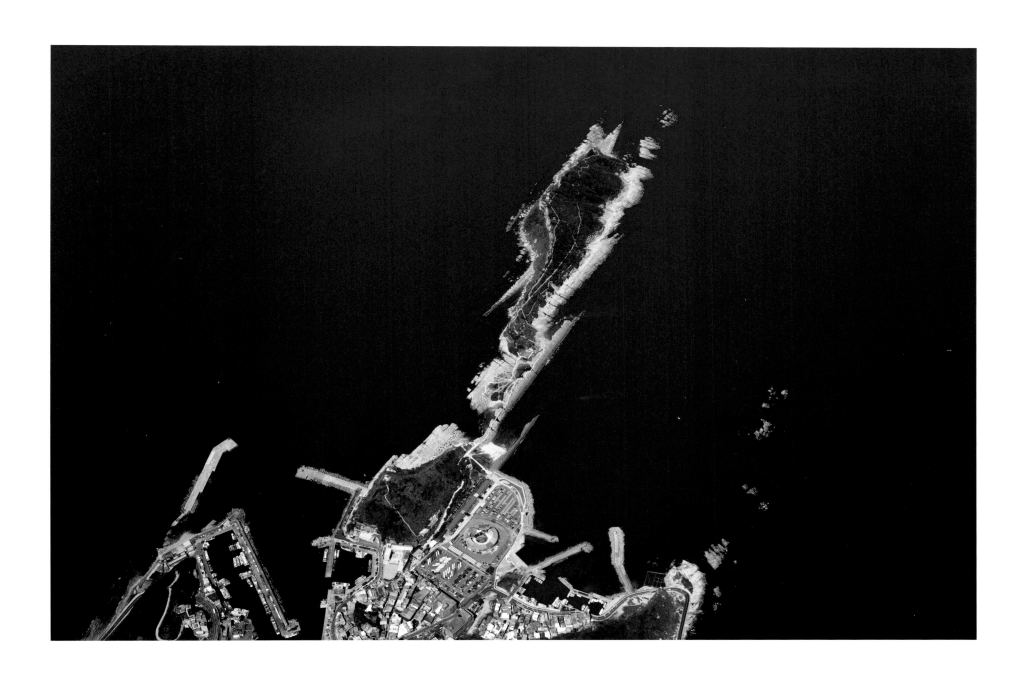

石雨傘海岸
Stone Umbrella
台東 Taitung 2011

約 1 公里長的石雨傘岬，為一砂岩海岬地形，海岬上方覆蓋了一層珊瑚礁，像是盔甲般保護岬角不受侵蝕，最為人熟知的海蝕地形是如雨傘般的「平衡岩」，為東海岸增添更多迷人的風情。

Shiyusan ("stone umbrella") Cape is a sandstone cape one kilometer in length. On top of the cape is a layer of coral, which protects it from the elements. The most famous coastal erosion landform here is the umbrella-like "balanced rocks," which only add to the east coast's charms.

小琉球

Xiaoliuqiu

屏東　Pingtung　2007

琉球嶼，俗稱小琉球，是屏東東港西南方的一座
珊瑚礁島嶼，屬大鵬灣國家風景區的一部分，是
台灣重要的珊瑚礁島嶼，孕育眾多潮間帶生物，
更有斷崖奇岩與無敵海景。

Liuqui Island, commonly known as Xiaoliuqiu, is a coral island southwest of Donggang, Pingtung. Part of the Dapeng Bay National Scenic Area, the island is a paradise rendered by the hand of God that features cliffs, oddly shaped rocks, and gorgeous seascapes.

鳥嶼砂尾
Bird Island Sand Spit
澎湖 Penghu 2008

位於澎湖群島東海的鳥嶼，由於洋流海積作用連結而成的一弧砂嘴地形，取名為澎澎灘，又因神似一尾活龍，也叫做活龍灘。

Located on the east side of the Penghu Archipelago, Bird Island features a sand spit named Pengpeng Beach, which is a deposition bar formed by sediment brought by ocean currents. Because it is shaped like a dragon, it is also called Dragon Beach.

目斗嶼燈塔

Mudouyu Lighthouse

澎湖　Penghu　2007

澎湖群島極北的目斗嶼，以黑白相間的美麗燈塔享極盛名，也是遠東地區最高的銑鐵燈塔，附近海溝猶如海底隧道，更為潛水客心目中的滄海遺世秘境。

Mudouyu is the northernmost island of the Penghu Archipelago and is famous for its beautiful lighthouse. Painted with black and white stripes, the lighthouse is the tallest cast-iron lighthouse in the Far East. The ocean trench nearby, a hidden gem for divers, resembles an undersea tunnel.

桃源谷、龜山島
The Taoyuan Historic Trail
and Guishan Island

宜蘭　Yilan　2011

桃源谷位於宜蘭與新北交界處，頂著北台灣第一美草原的頭銜，是淡蘭古道路網中的熱門健行路線之一，尤其臨海遠眺龜山島朦朧神韻，更添無限飄逸氛圍。

The Taoyuan Historic Trail is located where Yilan County meets New Taipei City. Passing through the most beautiful grasslands of northern Taiwan, it has become one of the most popular trails in the Danlan Historic Trail Network. Misty Guishan Island looks otherworldly from here.

阿朗壹古道

Alangyi Historic Trail

台東　Taitung　2009

台東達仁至屏東牡丹的阿朗壹古道，有台灣最美海岸線的稱號，在綿延起伏的山脈與浪潮不斷的太平洋之間，留存著台灣最後一哩的原始秘境。

The Alangyi Historic Trail, which leads from Daren, Taitung to Mudan, Pingtung, runs along Taiwan's most beautiful coastline. Winding between the undulating mountains and the surging Pacific, it offers views of some of Taiwan's last unspoiled stretches of coastline.

曾文溪口

The Zengwen River Estuary

台南　Tainan　2007

源於阿里山山脈的曾文溪，不僅有台灣最大的曾
文水庫，出海口更蔚為國際級溼地，亦納入台江
國家公園範圍內，這裡也是保育類動物黑面琵鷺
來台過冬的重要棲息地之一。

Originating at the Alishan Range, the Zengwen River feeds the biggest
reservoir in Taiwan and features world-class wetlands in its estuary. Part of
Taijiang National Park, the wetlands here serve as one of the important
winter habitats for endangered black-faced spoonbills.

大倉嶼

Dacangyu

澎湖　Penghu　2007

大倉嶼是澎湖本島、西嶼及白沙島環抱而成澎湖內海中的一座迷你小島，因而有「內海之珠」美稱，過去也是綠蠵龜頻繁出沒的歡樂天堂。

Dacangyu is a tiny islet surrounded by the islands of Penghu, Xiyu and Baisha. It is also known as the "Pearl of the Inner Sea." It used to be a place that green sea turtles frequented.

後壁湖海底珊瑚礁
Coral Reef, Houbi Lake

屏東　Pingtung　2011

屏東恆春的後壁湖，以裙礁地形猶如在地社區屋後的湖而得名，豐富的珊瑚礁和魚類生態歷歷在目，盡顯墾丁國家公園的海域風華。

Houbi means "behind the back wall." This fringing reef lagoon was so named because it looks like an ordinary lake behind a house. With an abundance of coral reefs and numerous fish, it provides a good window into the flourishing marine life of Kenting National Park.

花蓮溪出海口
Hualien River Estuary
花蓮　Hualien　2012

花蓮溪出海口除了緊鄰海岸山脈的北端起點，更
因溪水與洋流經年激盪，形成縈迴不已的巨浪與
沙嘴，古稱「洄瀾」，取其諧音，就這麼成了「花
蓮」的舊名。

The Hualien River Estuary is located at the northern
end of the Coastal Mountain Range. The impact of river
water hitting ocean currents creates huge waves and
sand spits here. The area was first known as Huilan,
which means "whirlpool of waves" in Chinese. "Huilan"
eventually became "Hualien."

芳苑濕地

The Fangyuan Wetland

彰化　Changhua　2010

彰化芳苑一帶海域濕地，具備特有的海牛採蚵人
文景觀，此種別具特色的濕地生態之旅，已不斷
躍上國際媒體舞台。

The wetlands in Changhua County's Fangyuan Township
feature a unique cultural heritage where carts
transporting harvested oysters are still pulled by oxen
in the traditional manner. In recent years, the unique
oxcart ecological wetland tours offered here have
received a lot of media attention internationally.

關渡紅樹林

Guandu's Mangrove Forest

新北　New Taipei　2015

關渡平原簇生著大面積的水筆仔紅樹林純林，由於感潮河段生物資源豐富，自然成為各種水鳥覓食與棲息的樂園，也是保育、教育、學術與遊憩的勝地。

With its large expanse of pristine mangrove forest and its rich tidal river ecological resources, Guandu's mangrove forest is a paradise for many species of water birds, which forage and rest here. It is also a great place for conservation work, education, academic research, and recreation.

龍井海岸濕地
Longjing Coastal Wetland
台中 Taichung 2008

台中龍井的大肚溪口野生動物保護區，兼有草澤
生態系與海岸生態系，水鳥密度和數量冠居全台，
早已被國際自然資源保育聯盟列為亞洲重要濕地
之一。

The Dadu River Mouth Wildlife Refuge in Taichung
City's Longjing features both marsh and coastal
ecosystems. In terms of both sheer numbers and
population density, there are more water birds here
than anywhere else in Taiwan. The refuge has been
listed as an important wetlands site in Asia by the
International Union for Conservation of Nature.

社子島泥灘地
Shezi Island Mudflats
台北 Taipei 2012

台北社子島拜基隆河與淡水河交匯之賜，具備獨特的泥灘溼地景觀，有招潮蟹、有彈塗魚、有紅樹林，當然還有人見人愛的飛羽嬌客。

Located at the confluence of the Keelung River and Tamsui River, Shezi Island has unique mudflats and mangrove forests that attract fiddler crabs, mudskippers, and many lovely water birds.

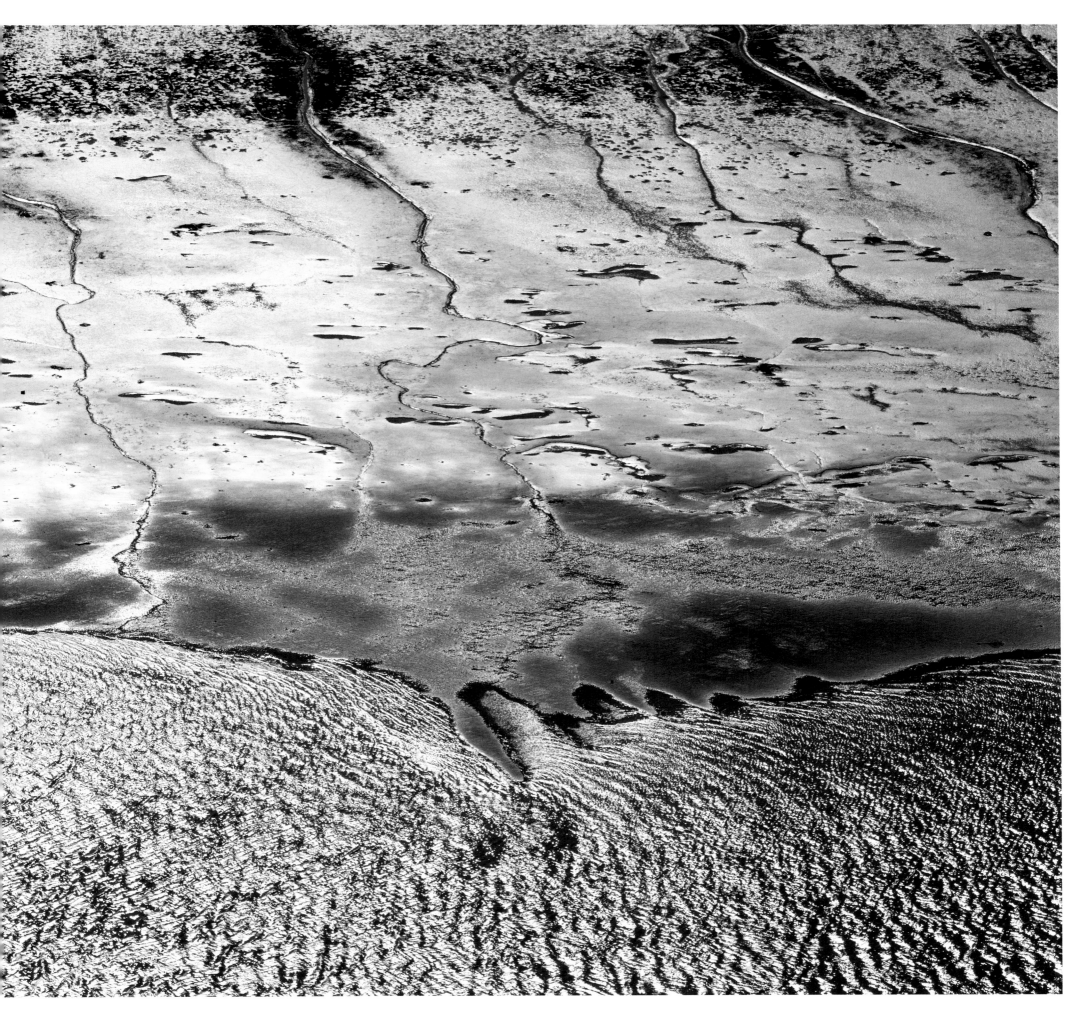

高美濕地

Gaomei Wetlands

台中 Taichung 2014

占地 700 多公頃的高美濕地，從日治時期的海水浴場，蛻變成為今日野生動物保護區，見證了滄海桑田的環境變遷，也詮釋了關懷自然的共識啟蒙。

A public beach during the Japanese era and today a wildlife refuge, the 700-hectare-plus Gaomei Wetlands have witnessed tremendous environmental change as well as a growing consensus to care for nature.

我常在空拍城市時找尋我家的地點，或許空拍是尋找另一個觀看「家」的角度。
別驚訝，這是我的心、我的眼，所看見的台灣，這片土地，是我們的家。

While shooting above the city, I often search for where I live, looking for another vantage point to see "home."

Don't be surprised to see Taiwan – this land that we all home – from my mind and my eyes.

齊柏林
Chi Po-lin

生 命 的 廣 度

The Breadth of Life

曲冰部落
Qubing Village

南投　Nantou　2005

曲冰部落位於南投縣仁愛鄉，行政地名為萬豐村，
屬布農族卓社群的原住民部落，1981 年曾有史前
聚落遺址出土，更令人嚮往的還是世外桃源般的
美樂地。

Qubing Village, officially known as Wanfeng Village, is
located in Renai Rural Township, Nantou County. This
Shangri-La is inhabited by members of the Bunun's
Takituduh community. In 1981, a prehistorical village
was unearthed here.

南山部落
Nanshan Village

宜蘭　Yilan　2011

宜蘭縣大同鄉的南山村，在蘭陽溪下切出的河階台地上，是泰雅族原鄉。

Located on a river terrace carved out by the Lanyang River, this village is home to the Atayal people.

秀姑巒溪曲流

Bends in the Xiuguluan River

花蓮　Hualien　2007

秀姑巒溪是台灣東部第一大河川，在縱谷中多條支流形成聯合沖積扇，並在奇美一帶由西向東切穿海岸山脈。此段河階迭起、曲流蜿蜒，美不勝收，更是東部著名的泛舟聖地。

The Xiuguluan River is the largest river in eastern Taiwan. Several of its branches create a coalescing alluvial fan in the rift valley. In the Qimei area, the river runs west to east and cuts through the Coastal Mountain Range, winding its way through many beautiful river terraces. It is a popular place to raft.

知本溪
Zhiben River
台東 Taitung 2010

台東知本溪發源自中央山脈霧頭山，一路往東注
入太平洋，流域所經的山地原鄉，盡顯桃花源般
的出塵美景。

Zhiben River originates from the Central Mountain
Range's Wutou Mountain. It flows east into the Pacific.
The beauty of the mountainous regions it flows
through is otherworldly.

隘寮北溪
Ailiao North River
屏東　Pingtung　2009

隘寮北溪屬荖濃溪支流，蜿蜒於屏東山地門與霧台境內，是形成屏東平原最大沖積扇的功臣，也是排灣族人心目中的母親之河。

Ailiao North River is a tributary of the Laonong River. Winding through Pingtung's Shandimen and Wutai, the river created the largest alluvial fan in the Pingtung Plain. The Paiwan people regard it as their "mother river."

羅娜部落

Louna Village

南投　Nantou　2007

信義鄉地扼中央山脈與玉山山脈之巔，面積冠居南投全境，而羅娜部落四周環境陡峭險峻，主為布農族人營生天地，也是台灣最大的原住民部落。

Xinyi Township is the largest township in Nantou County and home to the highest peaks of the Central Mountain Range and Yushan Range. The Bunun village of Louna, the largest indigenous village in Taiwan, is located in the township. It features a steep and perilous topography.

蘭嶼野銀部落
Yeyin Village, Orchid Island
台東　Taitung　2005

蘭嶼野銀部落鄰近東清灣，以達悟族傳統聚落馳
名，在這依山傍水、順應自然的世外桃源，猶保
存著遺世獨立的生活風情。

Located near Dongqing Bay on Orchid Island where
the mountains meet the sea, this Shangri-la-like Tao
village has maintained its traditional way of life.

太魯閣峽谷
Taroko Gorge
花蓮　Hualien　2011

花蓮立霧溪一手鐫刻出太魯閣傲世景觀，下游支流砂卡噹溪也林立著峽谷之美，不難想見，雲端之上的「黑暗部落」──大同部落，沒有體力與耐力實不足以抵達。

The Liwu River has carved out famous Taroko Gorge, but the Shakadang River, a tributary of the lower Liwu, is also blessed with magnificent canyon scenery. It is easy to see that it would require true physical fitness to reach lofty Datong Village, the renowned "Dark Village" near the Shakadang's headwaters.

蘭陽平原

Lanyang Plain

宜蘭 Yilan 2001

宜蘭蘭陽溪水系的沖積平原上，一畦又一畦的農田與魚塭，孕育出魚米之鄉的豐饒，以及醉人的山光水色。

Rice paddies and fish ponds are packed tightly into the alluvial plain of the Lanyang River system. The river supports rich harvests and offers charming scenery.

魚寮溪口海岸
Yuliao River Estuary
彰化　Changhua　2011

彰化大城位於濁水溪沖積扇平原最下游，魚寮溪
貫穿其間，由於河海交匯的潮間帶遍布泥質灘
地，是水鳥棲息天堂，大城濕地也因此成為台灣
賞鳥的一處熱點。

Dacheng is located on the Zuoshui River's alluvial
fan, where the Yuliao River cuts through. The tidal
mudflats in this estuary are a paradise for water
birds, which in turn draw bird watchers to the
Dacheng Wetlands.

蘭陽平原
Lanyang Plain
宜蘭 Yilan 2011

蘭陽平原三面環山，東濱太平洋，龜山島遙遙相
望，不僅有重巒疊翠的山水景致，還有安和樂利
的風土民情。

The Lanyang Plain is surrounded by mountains on three
sides with the Pacific Ocean and Guishan Island to its
east. It offers beautiful landscapes and scenery, as well
as rich and harmonious cultural traditions.

新岑里鹽場

Xincenli Salt Field

嘉義　Chiayi　2005

嘉義布袋曾以千甲鹽田，在台灣鹽業發展史中風光了近 200 年，隨著人工曬鹽走入歷史，今日代之而起的是鹽場人文及漁村景觀的巡禮。

Chiayi County's Budai Township was famous for its huge salt fields for nearly two centuries. With large-scale traditional salt production a thing of the past, today's visitors come for the fishing village and the salt field tours.

美濃全貌

Meinong

高雄　Kaohsiung　2006

高雄美濃地處荖濃溪沖積而成的沖積平原，是領略南台灣客家文化的寶庫，居民務農為主，過去曾經是台灣菸葉王國，今日響叮噹的農作物則為白玉蘿蔔。

Tucked amid mountains, Meinong is located on an alluvial plain created by sediment from the Laonong River. The town is a veritable treasure trove of Hakka culture in Southern Taiwan. The residents here are mainly farmers. Formerly a major tobacco producer, the town today is famous for its Daikon radishes.

九份

Jiufen

新北　New Taipei　2013

新北瑞芳的九份地區，以淘金歲月成就了山城名震一時的喧囂與繁華，雖然歷史演替難料，所幸，今日山與海的風光仍在，懷舊尋幽的人潮依然絡繹於途。

Jiufen, located in New Taipei City's Ruifang District, was once a prosperous gold mining town. Today, the charming hillside town attracts tourists who are looking to step back in time.

台北盆地

Taipei Basin

台北 Taipei 2010

台北盆地由大屯火山群、林口台地、雪山山脈與南港丘陵圍繞而成，行政上涵蓋台北市與新北市，是台灣最大的都會區，也是政經文教薈萃之地。

Taipei Basin is surrounded by Tatun Volcanic Group, Linkou Mesa, Xueshan Range, and Nangang Hills. Administratively, the basin falls within the boundaries of Taipei City and New Taipei City. Taipei is the largest metropolitan area in Taiwan.

台北 101 山嵐
Taipei 101 in Mountain Mist
台北 Taipei 2013

台北 101 以台灣第一摩天大樓英姿，鶴立在群山
環抱的台北盆地中，象徵的不僅止於國際金融地
標的體現，更是努力追求與在地環境共榮的驕傲。

The tallest building in Taiwan and a landmark of international finance,
Taipei 101 embodies efforts to proudly combine prosperity with
environmentalism.

壽山
Shoushan
高雄　Kaohsiung　2013

壽山俗稱柴山，是高雄臨海地區的天然屏障，地質上屬隆起珊瑚礁石灰岩，天然岩洞甚多，並保有完整而獨立的生態體系，可謂高雄的都市之肺。

Shoushan, commonly known in English as Monkey Mountain, is a natural barrier along the coast of Kaohsiung. Geologically formed by calcium carbonate from coral reefs, it features many natural caves and has a fully independent ecosystem. It is regarded as "the lungs of Kaohsiung."

青鯤鯓

Qingkunshen

台南 Tainan　年代不詳　Undated

台南青鯤鯓鹽田肇建於 1975 年，以扇形開展外觀博得台灣最美鹽田稱號，雖然曬鹽任務在 1991 年終止，仍絲毫無損大地紋理之美的吸睛特色。

Established in 1975, Tainan's Qingkunshen Salt Field is regarded as the most beautiful salt field in Taiwan because of its fan-shaped appearance. Though it stopped producing salt in 1991, its beauty remains undimmed.

長濱梯田

Terraced Paddy Fields in Changbin

台東　Taitung　2011

台東長濱依山傍海，境內「梯田大道」的綠浪景觀，滿是遊子慕名追焦的足跡，而在地擁有太平洋味道的「海稻米」，更是阿美族部落守護家鄉、守護傳統的生活寄託。

Changbin is a rural township in Taitung surrounded with mountains and sea. The green landscape within the "terrace avenue" always attracts many travelers to visit, and the "sea rice" that is filled with the taste of the Pacific Ocean reflects the lifestyles of the indigenous Amis tribe to keep their homeland and traditions.

網室農業

Net House Agriculture

雲林　Yunlin　2010

嘉南平原是台灣最大的穀倉，雲林西螺除了膾炙人口的西螺大橋與老街美食外，也因濁水溪孕育出萬頃良田，蔬菜、稻米與醬油等特產馳名遠近。

The Jianan Plain is "the granary of Taiwan." Its Xiluo Township in Yunlin County is famous for its Xiluo Bridge and the gourmet snacks of its "Old Street," as well as for its soy sauce, its vegetables and the rice grown in its broad expanses of rice paddies.

新板特區

New Banqiao District

新北　New Taipei　2012

台北盆地水系發達，自古以來一直都是北台灣歷史與文明重鎮，而新板特區急遽發展，也在新北市的版圖鞏立中占有重要地位。

Taipei Basin, with its many rivers, has a long history of human settlement. Its New Banciao Station Special District has been rapidly developing and lies at the heart of New Taipei City.

我認為，所謂的愛就是一種默默地陪伴守候，不管是對家人還是這片土地。

I believe that what we call "love" describes a kind of unspoken supportive companionship, whether it is directed toward one's family or toward the land.

齊柏林
Chi Po-lin

土　　地　　的　　溫　　度

The Warmth of the Land

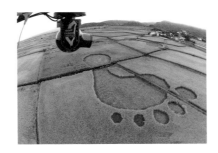

田園景觀

Farm Landscape

雲林 Yunlin 2012

雲林是台灣著名的農業大縣，元長鄉以栽種花生著稱，產量台灣第一，尤其「黑金剛」花生風味特殊，是相當知名的伴手禮。

Yunlin County is one of Taiwan's major agricultural counties. Its Yuanzhang Rural Township boasts the largest peanut production on the island. The town's uniquely flavored "Black Kingkong" peanuts have become popular souvenirs.

苑裡農田

Yuanli Farmland

苗栗　Miaoli　2012

苑裡是苗栗西南隅的一個小鎮，有「苗栗穀倉」之譽，並以百年傳承的藺草編織馳名，近年來為搶救淺山活動的石虎族群，友善耕作的「石虎米」也蔚為風潮。

Yuanli, known as the "Granary of Miaoli," is a small town nestled in the southwest corner of Miaoli County. It is famous for its rush weaving, which has been an important craft here for a century. In recent years, local conservationists have been striving to keep leopard cats active in the lower-elevation slopes nearby. The "Leopard Cat Rice" grown using wildlife-friendly farming practices here has become very popular.

農民插秧

Transplanting Rice Seedlings

彰化　Changhua　2009

插秧時，必須小心翼翼將培育好的秧苗移植田中，這是栽種水稻很重要的過程，打好基礎，才能順利成長。

Transplanting rice seedlings is a very important step in growing rice—one that farmers must do with great care. Rice will only flourish with strong roots.

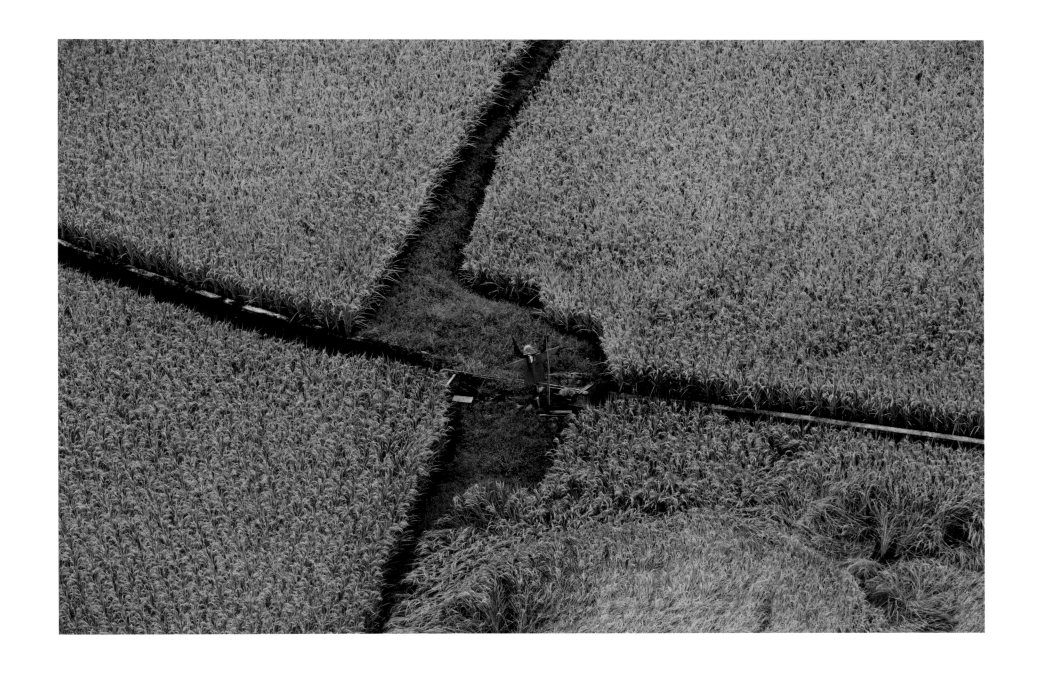

紅色稻草人
Red Scarecrow

花蓮　Hualien　2012

矗立稻田之中的稻草人，主要是為了防止鳥類擾
亂農作物，成為田間十分有趣的裝置藝術。

Scarecrows exist to prevent birds from damaging crops and serve as interesting works of installation art in the rice paddies.

西瓜田

Fields of Watermelons

屏東　Pingtung　2008

西瓜是台灣的重要水果農產之一，性喜高溫，又需土質排水透氣良好，河床砂丘與沿海砂地最適宜生長。

Watermelons are an important agricultural crop in Taiwan. They prefer high temperatures and well-drained light soils. In Taiwan, they are best grown in dunes along riverbeds or coastlines.

新武呂溪
Xinwulu River

台東 Taitung 2011

過去在稻田收割後，農民習慣露天焚燒稻草以防治病蟲害，並當作土壤的肥料。為了避免燃燒稻草造成空氣汙染，如今鼓勵改採就地掩埋的方式處置。

After the harvest, farmers used to burn rice stalks in the open air to kill insects, prevent disease and fertilize the soil. To prevent air pollution, farmers are now instead being encouraged to bury the rice stalks in situ.

插秧的稻田
Seedlings in Rice Paddies

台中　Taichung　2016

台灣的稻作屬水稻品種，插秧期間需要足夠的灌溉水源，整齊有序的稻田與秧苗，正是豐年的象徵。

Taiwan's rice is paddy rice, so the fields need to be flooded during the transplantation of seedlings. Managing this process in an orderly manner is a harbinger of a good harvest.

高鐵列車
Taiwan High Speed Rail Trains

雲林 Yunlin 2012

二崙地處雲林最北緣，一眼望去盡是平疇沃野，尤以稻米、西瓜與香瓜等農特產馳名，台灣高鐵亦於境內橫越阡陌，為旅程添景生色。

Located at the northern edge of Yunlin County, Erlun is well-known for its agricultural products such as rice, watermelons, and melons. When Taiwan high speed Rail trains traverse Erlun, the sweeping views of beautiful farmland make for an enjoyable trip.

黃土蘿蔔田

Daikon Radish Fields

台中　Taichung　2011

台灣蘿蔔品種繁多，也是鮮食與加工的重要農特
產品，一望無際的蘿蔔田，看見土地的豐饒、看
見農業發展的好「彩頭」。

There are many cultivars of Daikon radish grown in Taiwan. In Taiwan, they
represent an important crop, sold in fresh markets and used in processed
foods. Boundless expanses of daikon radish fields bear witness to the
land's fertility and offer good omens for the future of agriculture (since the
Chinese name for "daikon radish" is a homonym for "good omen").

稻田裡的大腳印
Footprints in the Rice Paddies

花蓮 Hualien 2012

稻田始終是台灣相當精彩的農業景觀，無論是成長期的碧綠或收割時的金黃，在在令人萬分感動。

Taiwan's rice paddies always present marvelous vistas—whether the lush green of the growing season or the golden yellow of harvest.

巡田水
Inspecting Water Levels

嘉義 Chiayi 2009

水稻種植，灌溉排水的系統非常重要，插秧後的
稻田必須確認水位足夠生長所需。

Managing irrigation and drainage is of utmost importance when it comes
to the growing of rice. After the seedlings are transplanted, farmers need to
make sure there is enough water in the paddies.

地瓜收成
Harvesting Sweet Potatoes

台中 Taichung 2009

番薯是最貼近台灣鄉土記憶的農作物，無論台農 57 號黃肉地瓜或台農 66 號紅肉地瓜，每一畝收成都是汗水與淚水交織的樂章。

The sweet potato is a form of agricultural produce tightly connected with the Taiwanese people's collective memories of the land. For every acre harvested—whether of Tainong 57 yellow flesh sweet potatoes or of Tainong 66 red flesh sweet potatoes—much sweat and tears are shed.

關山稻田
Rice Paddies in Guanshan

台東　Taitung　2008

台東關山以「關山米」馳名遠近，是花東縱谷的稻米之鄉，稻田洋溢豐富的線條與顏彩，彷彿大自然的調色盤。

Guanshan, a large rice producer in the East Rift Valley, is famous for its "Guanshan Rice." The rice paddies here feature "nature's color palette."

關山電光里梯田
Guanshan Dianguangli Rice Terraces

台東 Taitung 2008

因應坡地地形而開闢的水稻梯田，以北台灣較見分布，花東縱谷的電光社區，梯田規模近 200 公頃，每每成為攝影追焦的熱門場域。

Rice terraces are constructed to make better use of a sloped terrain. In Taiwan, they are more common in the north. Dianguang Village in the East Rift Valley has nearly 200 hectares of rice terraces. It is a popular spot for photos.

蛤蠣採收

Harvesting Clams

台中 Taichung 2011

蛤蠣，俗稱文蛤，是台灣最受歡迎的海水養殖貝類，雖然機器化篩選和分級可以節省人力，但漁民期盼的卻是，今年的收成足不足以養活一家人？

The clam is the most popular marine culture mollusk in Taiwan. The use of machines to sort grades can help to save labor, but there is one question that preoccupies these fishermen: Will this year's hauls be enough to feed their families?

海牛採蚵
Transporting Harvested Oysters with Oxcarts

彰化 Changhua 2012

黃牛犁田或許是早年農村普見的景象，但在彰化芳苑，漁民駕著黃牛採蚵，道盡以海為生的智慧，可謂世界級的漁村人文景觀。

Oxen plowing fields used to be a common sight in Taiwan, but the past lives on in Changhua County's Fangyuan Township, where fishermen drive oxcarts to haul oysters. This image of fishing village life constitutes a world-class cultural sight and bears witness to the wisdom that these men have gained from the sea.

魚塭夕陽

Sunset over Fish Ponds

高雄　Kaohsiung　2011

高雄臨海北側的茄萣一帶，早年有大片潟湖濕地，
如今已變身成為水產養殖重鎮，為地方產業發展
增添了更多的光輝。

The area around Qieding at the northern end of Kaohsiung's coastline used
to have expansive lagoon wetlands. Today the wetlands have become an
important center of fish farming, adding to the bounty of local production.

魚塭、蚵田
Fish and Oyster Farms

雲林 Yunlin 2011

雲林口湖克服地層下陷的積水,改以成龍濕地知名,並因舉辦國際環境藝術節而享譽國際。在此,無論蚵田或魚塭,處處是生態之美、處處有人文之景。

When the farm lands here became waterlogged as a result of land subsidence, Yunlin's Kouhu changed course and became known for its Chenglong Wetlands. The township's International Environmental Art Project is famous globally. Here, cultural and ecological beauty can be found at oyster and fish farms alike.

大鵬灣
Dapeng Bay

屏東　Pingtung　年代不詳　Undated

屏東大鵬灣是國家風景區所在地，為一潟湖濕地，除紅樹林生態可觀，湖域附近以浮動的箱網養殖牡蠣，數大就是美。

Designated as a national scenic area, Dapeng Bay is a lagoon whose mangrove forests provide habitat for many species. Near the bay, oyster farmers raise oysters in floating cases. Here large numbers equate with beauty.

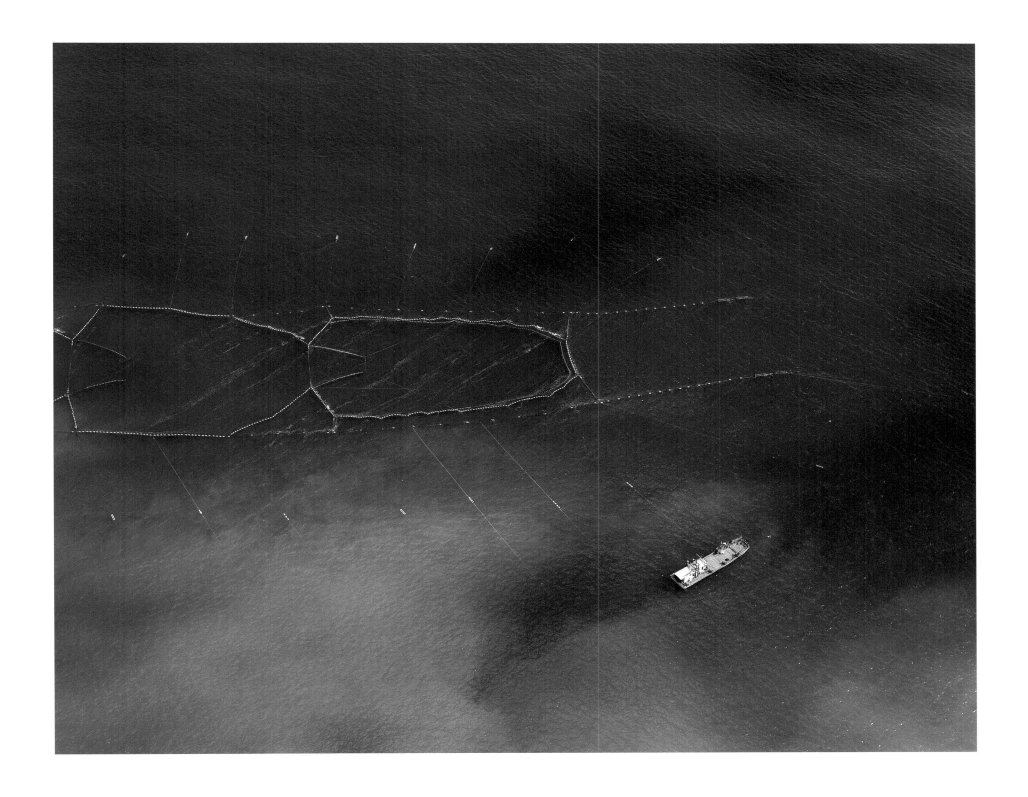

定置漁場

Fixed-Net Fishing

花蓮　Hualien　2004

定置漁業是一種古老的漁撈作業方法，利用沿岸海流引魚群進入漁網陷阱，雖然收穫難以預期，但對大海而言，較不會有竭澤而漁的傷害。

Fixed-net fishing is an ancient method. It makes use of ocean currents to lure fish into nets. Though hauls may be hard to predict, the method is less likely to deplete the ocean of fish.

蚵架
Oyster Racks

台南 Tainan 2014

台南北門一帶海域，因具備廣大潮間帶環境，牡蠣養殖採固定式棚架，「海中的牛奶」隨著潮起潮落而開閉，一暝大一吋。

Highly nutritious, oysters are called the "milk of the sea" in Taiwan. There are large expanses of tidal flats off Beimen in Tainan, where oysters, farmed using fixed racks, grow very quickly.

台灣海峽輪船
Boat in Taiwan Strait

苗栗 Miaoli 2011

台灣海峽位於亞洲及太平洋之間，早期有「黑水溝」之稱，是台灣先民渡海移墾的渠道，也是東亞水域經貿往來的要衝。

The Taiwan Strait is located between China and the Pacific Ocean. It was the "Black Ditch" that pioneering Han Chinese settlers of Taiwan had to cross from the mainland, and it remains an important segment of East Asian trading routes.

在九二一之後，我大規模拍攝了台灣山林的變化，處處都是滑動的土石，蓊鬱的山林常常就中間滑掉了一大片，留下醜陋的土黃色。

我原本認為，台灣的山只有兩種顏色，一種是白雪的白，一種是常年的綠，現在多了第三種，是滿山遍野、殘破的土黃色，像是大地的傷口。

After the earthquake of September 21, 1999, I documented extensively the changes to Taiwan's mountain forests. Everywhere were piles of earth and rocks from landslides.

Amid the lush forest, one would suddenly see a large landslide that had left an ugly gash upon the earth. At first I believed that Taiwan's mountains had only two colors:

the white of snow and the evergreen of plants. Now there was a third: the yellow-brown color of earth found everywhere in the mountains that represents wounds upon the land.

齊柏林
Chi Po-lin

和　　諧　　的　　限　　度

The Limits of Harmony

南 投
Nantou

南投九九峰擁有如火炎般的特殊地理景觀，1999
年集集大地震之後，大量植被隨土石崩坍，造成
山頭裸露。

99 Peaks in Nantou has a unique fiery look to it. After
the 1999 Jiji Earthquake, landslides wiped out large
expanses of vegetation, leaving a naked mountain top.

1999

雲 林
Yunlin

雲林古坑的草嶺地區，過去常因山崩而攔截清水
溪形成堰塞湖，1999 年集集地震後一度出現台灣
面積最大的天然湖泊，但 2004 年 72 水災後，草
嶺潭又消失了。

Landslides have often blocked Qingshui Creek and
formed barrier lakes in the Caoling area of Yunlin's
Gukeng. After the 1999 Jiji Earthquake, Taiwan's largest
natural lake was created here, but it disappeared when
flooding on July 2, 2004 washed out its debris dam.

南投
Nantou

2001 年 7 月 30 日桃芝颱風來襲，南投水里的三部坑溪上游挾帶大量土石傾瀉而下，造成下游的上安村橋斷路毀、房舍倒塌，以冬季賞梅聞名的美麗田園嚴重受創。

Kaohsiung's Liugui has a beautiful topography with rift valleys and alluvial fans. River rafting on its Laonong River has become popular with tourists. But flooding associated with Typhoon Morakot in 2009 brought rocks and mud that covered the green hillsides, completely burying Xinkai Village by the river.

2001　　　　　　2005　　　　　　　　　　　　　　　　　　　2006

桃園
Taoyuan

2005 年 10 月 10 日，載運有毒液態苯的韓籍化學輪船「三和兄弟號」（The Samho Brother），在桃園永安外海遭賴比瑞亞籍貨輪追撞，後於 12 月 27 日採空中炸射方式將之擊沉。

Off Taoyuan´s Yongan on October 10, 2005, the Samho Brother, a Korean chemical tanker carrying toxic liquid benzene, collided with a Liberian freighter. On December 27, it sank after being aerially bombed.

南投
Nantou

南投大清境社區所在地，是一片高冷蔬果園與民宿區。然而，山區較為敏感的環境，面對人們的超限利用，潛在的風險似乎離我們並不遙遠。

Nantou's Daqingjing Community is full of high-altitude vegetable farms, orchards and homestays. The mountains, however, are sensitive environments. Problems caused by overuse make the dangers inherent to these locations only more severe.

南投
Nantou

南投仁愛鄉翠巒部落以高山茶享名，也同樣面臨台灣高山茶園過度開發的課題，只要逢連日大雨，就要擔心土石滑落、產業道路受阻的困境。

Known for its tea, the Cuiluan tribal village in Nantou's Ren'ai Rural Township is facing the problem of excessive development of mountain slopes for tea production. Consecutive days of strong rains always raise fears about landslides that could block road access.

颱風帶來強降雨，往往對山坡地造成致命的傷害，2006 年 7 月 13 日碧利斯颱風肆虐台灣，南投霧社山區但見土石泥流崩傾下滑，觸目驚心。

Typhoons bring heavy rains that can often wreak deadly havoc on mountain slopes. On July 13, 2006 Tropical Storm Bilis battered Taiwan, offering this shocking scene of mudslides and rockslides in action at Wushe, Nantou.

台中
Taichung

台 8 線中橫公路橫亙台灣中央山脈，曾經是人定勝天的工程奇蹟，但由於沿線地質極度不穩，容易受天候影響而落石坍方，1999 年集集地震後更見滿目瘡痍。

Once regarded as an engineering marvel, Provincial Highway 8 (the Central Cross-Island Highway) crosses Taiwan's Central Mountain Range. Because the slopes along it are unstable, bad weather frequently causes falling rocks and landslides. It was devastated by the 1999 Jiji Earthquake.in Taiwan's cities.

2006   **2008**   **2009**

苗栗
Miaoli

苗栗三義的火炎山，長年受大安溪溪水切割，加上侵蝕與崩塌作用，礫岩惡地景觀無比壯麗，且有大面積的馬尾松林生態，於 1986 年劃為自然生態保留區。

Mt. Huoyen in Miaoli has been shaped by the Daan River. The erosion and slope collapse have created a magnificent gravelly landscape. Furthermore, it also features large expanses of Masson pines. In 1986, it was officially designated as a nature preserve.

高雄
Kaohsiung
2009 年 8 月 8 日莫拉克颱風為南台灣帶來驚人雨勢，高屏溪支流荖濃溪在六龜至寶來河段也造成大量土石崩塌，知名溫泉區與宗教聖地一夕之間山河變色。

On August 8, 2009, Typhoon Morakot brought alarming rainfalls to southern Taiwan. The Laonong River, which is a tributary of the Kaoping River, experienced significant mud and rockslides along the stretch from Liugui to Baolai. The space between the river and the ridges, famous for its hot springs and temples, was changed overnight.

高雄
Kaohsiung
2009 年 8 月 8 日莫拉克颱風來襲，高雄甲仙地區的獻肚山不堪豪大雨侵襲，大量走山滑落的土石崩坍，造成小林村 100 多戶人家，就此消失在故鄉的山腳下。

With the arrival of Typhoon Morakot on August 8, 2009, Mt. Xiandu in the Jiaxian District of Kaohsiung experienced unbearably high rainfall. The resulting landslides caused Xiaolin, a village of more than 100 households at the foot of the mountain, to completely disappear.

2009

高雄
Kaohsiung
高雄六龜有秀麗的縱谷與台地沖積扇地形，並以荖濃溪泛舟活動廣受遊客青睞，但 2009 年莫拉克風災無情肆虐，土石流吞沒了青翠山巒，也掩埋了溪岸的新開部落。

Kaohsiung's Liugui has a beautiful topography with rift valleys and alluvial fans. River rafting on its Laonong River has become popular with tourists. But flooding associated with Typhoon Morakot in 2009 brought rocks and mud that covered the green hillsides, completely burying the Hsinkai village the Hsinkai village (an aboriginal tribe) along the river.

台東
Taitung

水泥消波塊有海邊的「肉粽角」之稱，因為巨大又笨重，所以經常用來保護海岸。然而，這些消波塊阻隔了波浪的同時，也阻隔了生態，以及人們親近大海的心。

Concrete tetrapods have been called "coastal rice dumplings." Huge and heavy, they are often employed to help protect the coastline. Yet, while these tetrapods shield the coastline, they also disrupt ecologies and keep people away from the sea.

雲林
Yunlin

設址於雲林麥寮的台塑六輕，對於穩定台灣石化原料的供給功不可沒，也是離島型工業區的成功典範，但廠區排放物影響空氣品質及居民健康的環保爭議始終不斷。

Taiwan's Sixth Naphtha Cracker Plant, which is located in Yunlin County's Mailiao, has made an important contribution toward stabilizing Taiwan's supply of petrochemicals, and it has served as a model for locating industrial plants offshore. But the impact of its emissions on air quality and local residents' health has been a constant source of controversy ever since it opened.

 2010

2011

高雄
Kaohsiung

高雄小港與林園交界的駱駝山，屬珊瑚礁地質，日治時期曾經是台灣重要的石灰產區，雖然事過境遷，但還是可以看到環境脆弱的一面。

Located between Kaohsiung's Xiaogang and Linyuan, Camel Mountain has a geology created by coral reefs. During the Japanese era, it was an important center of lime production in Taiwan. Although the industry has moved on, it has left a fragile-looking landscape.

花蓮
Hualien

花蓮和仁水泥礦場提供地方產業經濟一條發展的路，卻也在一片秀麗的後山原鄉中，突兀地形成大面積的「梯田」與「斷頭山」景觀。

The cement quarries in Hualien's Heren offer opportunities for economic development, but they also have left ugly vistas of "fill terraces" and "topless mountains" in what is otherwise a beautiful backcountry mountain landscape.

高雄
Kaohsiung

台灣以惡地特殊景觀馳名的月世界，主要分布在高雄、台南一帶，雖然舉目所見盡是一片荒漠，不利農事耕種，卻也有人另謀他途，在坡地間蓄水闢建出一池池魚塘。

"Moon World" is a striking stretch of badlands in Kaohsiung and Tainan. Although it appears to be a barren expanse that is ill-suited to the cultivation of crops, people have found a way to make the land productive by building fish ponds on the slopes here.

2012

新北
New
Taipei

由於地狹人稠，台灣居大不易，許多房舍屋頂上都可以見到違章建築，尤其施工快、重量輕，又相對造價低的「鐵皮屋」更是見怪不怪。

Because land is limited and people numerous, makeshift illegal penthouses—especially metal panel structures, which are light, quickly built and cheap—are common in Taiwan's cities.

台東
Taitung

莫拉克颱風八八風災重創南台灣，源自中央山脈南段主峰北大武山、南大武山的太麻里溪，也因為受到走山崩坍而形成堰塞湖。

Typhoon Morakot battered southern Taiwan with strong winds and rain that caused landslides. Where Taimali Creek had flowed between the north and south peaks of Mt. Dawu at the southern end of the Central Mountain Range, a new barrier lake was created.

2013　　　　　　　　　　　　　　　　　　　　　　　　　　2015

高雄
Kaohsiung

高雄阿公店溪源自烏山，總長約 38 公里，曾經名列第一，台灣最嚴重汙染河川，而且從生活廢水、事業廢水到畜牧廢水都有。

Kaohsiung's Agongdian River starts on Wushan and stretches for 38 kilometers. It was once Taiwan's most polluted river. Residential and industrial sewage, as well as livestock waste water, all contributed to its filth.

桃園
Taoyuan

大崛溪從桃園觀音注入台灣海峽，上游有楊梅幼獅工業區，下游又與觀音工業區為鄰，一條小溪實在承受不了工業汙水長年不當排放的壓力。

The Dajue River enters the Taiwan Strait at Guanyin in Taoyuan. The Youth Industrial Park in Yangmei sits on the upper stretches of the river, and downstream the river is close to the Guanyin Industrial Park. In reality, one small river cannot be expected to bear the pressures of such long-term pollution.

嘉義
Chiayi

一片朦朧山水景觀，看似唯美，有時卻是不期而來的空氣汙染，霧霾具懸浮微粒，對身體健康有不良影響，尤其冬日常伴隨大陸冷氣團南下，出現在台灣西部天空。

Misty landscapes may look dreamy, but sometimes the mist is actually smog created by particulate air pollution, which is bad for human health. During winter in particular, smog often forms along Taiwan's west coast as cold fronts move south from mainland China.

2015

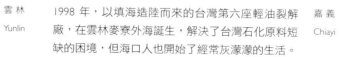

雲林
Yunlin

1998 年，以填海造陸而來的台灣第六座輕油裂解廠，在雲林麥寮外海誕生，解決了台灣石化原料短缺的困境，但海口人也開始了經常灰濛濛的生活。

Taiwan's Sixth Naptha Cracker Plant was opened on landfill just off the coast of Yunlin's Mailiao in 1998. It solved the problem of shortages for certain petrochemicals, but it has made coastal smog a frequent part of daily life there.

嘉義
Chiayi

水漾森林是嘉義的新興景點，夢幻一如仙境，究其成因，竟是 1999 年集集大地震當時，因山崩阻塞石鼓盤溪所形成的堰塞湖。

The Shuiyang Forest, with its dreamlike landscapes, is a new attraction in Chiayi. It features a barrier lake, which was created by landslides during the 1999 Jiji Earthquake. The debris impeded the flow of the Shigupan Creek.

2013 年，《看見台灣》電影播出之後，馬英九政府成立「國土保育專案小組」，研究和改善 16 項有關環境保育的議題，
2017 年 6 月 24 日，蔡英文總統出席《看見齊柏林》紀念展頒發褒揚令，呼籲「看見台灣，珍惜土地」，
並允諾未來政府將延續齊柏林的精神，持續推動國土復育工作。

齊柏林終其一生，用鏡頭告訴我們台灣土地的故事、用生命提醒我們環境保護的重要。

凝視齊柏林，我們看見了台灣的國土變遷樣貌、見證了環境發展過程中重要的事件與里程。

In 2013, after Beyond Beauty: Taiwan from Above was released, ROC President Ma Ying-jeou established a National Land Conservation Taskforce to study about 16 environmental issues and effect change.
Then on June 24, 2017, ROC President Tsai Ing-wen presented a presidential citation to honor Chi Po-lin at a memorial exhibition of his work. She called for the public "to see Taiwan and to treasure the land"
and promised to honor Chi's spirit by continuing to push for environmental restoration.

Throughout his life, Chi used his lens to tell stories about Taiwan. He lived his life reminding us about the importance of protecting the environment.

Looking at Chi Po-lin and his work, we see how the land of Taiwan has been changing, and we become witnesses to important incidents and milestones in its evolution.

左： 核三廠出水口、小巴厘島岩

Left: Water outlet of the 3rd Nuclear Power Plant, Little Bali Rock

屏東　Pingtung　2017.06.09

右： 高雄港港區污染

Right: Pollution of Kaohsiung Harbor

高雄　Kaohsiung　2017.06.09

最 後 的 凝 視 (2017.6.9)

The Last Gaze (2017.6.9)

看見·齊柏林基金會
Chi Po-lin Foundation

為完成齊柏林導演未竟之志，由齊導摯友、親人共同發起，於 2018 年 2 月正式成立「財團法人看見·齊柏林基金會」，並以「永續、扎根、傳承、志業」為宗旨。

透過數位典藏計畫，有系統保存台灣地景地貌的脈動，運用影像作品推廣環境教育理念，持續深耕土地，延續齊導「看見台灣、守護家園」的精神。

未來，基金會將發揮守望環境的功能，喚起國人對於捍衛生存環境的覺醒，讓每個世代都能把對島嶼的愛與關懷內化為堅定的信念，為這塊土地積極尋找下一個齊柏林。

To achieve Chi Po-lin's unrealized aspiration, his close friends and family founded Chi Po-lin Foundation in February 2018, making "sustainability, education, legacy and vocation" the objectives.

The Foundation adopts a digital collection program to systematically preserve the images of Taiwan's topography and landscape while employing the valuable images to promote environmental education, creating a lasting positive influence in the island and continuing Chi's spirit of "Perceiving Taiwan, Preserving Home."

The Foundation will endeavor in guarding the environment and raise more awareness of protecting our living environment. By doing so, the love and care for this island from each of the future generations will be transformed into a strong belief and more people like Chi Po-lin can be expected in the future.

齊柏林空間
CHI PO-LIN MUSEUM

2019 年 4 月，由財團法人看見·齊柏林基金會所發起，落腳於淡水得忌利士洋行的「齊柏林空間」正式揭幕。

齊柏林空間集結空拍攝影大師齊柏林導演生前的影像作品，結合在地人文特色，構築成聚焦台灣故事的影像基地與築夢平台，向世界宣揚台灣友善土地、保護環境與關懷生命的真諦。

透過線上的深化典藏與線下的永續經營，齊柏林空間將持續與國內外關注生態環境保護的影像創作者交流、合作與對話；期望能在展現島嶼魅力之餘，亦能在環境保護政策上發揮影響力，成為兼具展望性與使命感的場域。

Inaugurated in April 2019, Chi Po-lin Museum is founded by Chi Po-lin Foundation and located in Douglas Lapraik & Co. in Tamsui.

The museum features photographic and video works by aerial photography master and filmmaker, Chi Po-lin, and serves as an image base and a dream-making platform incorporated with local and cultural features and dedicated to the stories of Taiwan. Its goal is to promote the meanings of cherishing the land, protecting the environment and caring for life and spread them from Taiwan to the globe.

Through consistently strengthening collection online and ensuring sustainably operation with concrete efforts, Chi Po-lin Museum aims to continuously engage Taiwanese and foreign photographers and filmmakers who dedicate their careers to environmental protection in exchanges, collaborations and dialogues. It is our hope to both unfold the charismatic charm of this beautiful island and effect positive changes in formulating policies concerning environmental issues, making this museum a site of vision and mission.

齊柏林　年表

1964　出生於台北市。

1990　服務公職後，開始負責空拍各項重大工程的興建過程。

1998　於《大地地理》雜誌發表空中攝影作品。

2003　獲第一屆 Johnnie Walker「The Keep Walking Fund 夢想資助計畫」。

2005　擔任奧比斯基金會的光明大使代言人，參與新疆救盲任務 。

2009　籌拍《看見台灣》電影紀錄片。

2011　參與公共電視「想。飛台灣 Free Your Mind 」短片，獲金鐘獎頻道廣告獎。

2012　獲第 4 屆學學獎 (Xue Xue Awards) 特殊貢獻獎。

　　　發表《鳥目台灣》空拍紀錄短片。

　　　個人短片《Google Search 搜尋故事—齊柏林篇》。

2013　《看見台灣》紀錄片電影上映，全台票房累積 2 億 2 仟萬。

　　　《看見台灣》榮獲第 50 屆金馬獎最佳紀錄片獎項 。

　　　《飛閱臺灣國家公園》空拍影片獲美國第 46 屆休士頓世界影展
　　　（ WorldFest-Houston International Film Festival) 金牌獎 。

　　　發表《我的心，我的眼，看見台灣 : 齊柏林空拍 20 年的堅持與深情 》。

　　　執行高雄市政府都市發展局《飛閱高雄》影片。

　　　執行臺中市政府新聞局《台中心動》影片。

2014　《看見台灣》榮獲第 21 屆國際綠色影展金太陽獎 。

　　　《看見台灣》榮獲第 47 屆休士頓國際影展劇情長度紀錄片評審團特別獎、攝影金牌獎 。

　　　與豐華唱片合作舉辦「看見台灣跨界音樂會」。

　　　與空軍救護隊合作完成《看見臺灣—慈航天使》微電影。

　　　獲選為國家地理台灣探險家。

2015　獲《影像的力量》中國（ 大同 ）國際攝影文化展攝影師至高榮譽「鏡美尊」稱號 。

　　　執行桃園市政府農業局《遇見桃園》影片。

2016　獲中華民國國軍文藝傑出貢獻獎。

　　　個人短片《Home Run Movie—看見齊柏林》。

2017　6 月 8 日舉辦《看見台灣 II》開鏡記者會。

　　　6 月 10 日於花蓮執行《看見台灣 II》空中拍攝任務時，不幸罹難。

　　　6 月 24 日獲頒總統褒揚令。

　　　個人短片《ZEISS Fascinating Fans—齊柏林導演》。

　　　看見·齊柏林基金會成立。

2019　齊柏林空間落成。

Chi Po-lin: Timeline

1964   Born in Taipei.

1990   After taking a government job, he begins taking aerial photographs of the construction process of major works of infrastructure.

1998   His aerial photographs appear in *The Good Earth Magazine*.

2003   Recipient of Johnnie Walker's inaugural Keep Walking Award.

2005   Orbis International, an international organization that fights blindness, appoints Chi to be a spokesperson for their "Flying Eye Hospital Mission" in Xinjiang, China.

2009   He makes plans to shoot *Beyond Beauty: Taiwan from Above*.

2011   His short *Fly to Taiwan. Free Your Mind* for PTS wins a Golden Bell Award.

2012   At the 4th Xue Xue Awards, he garners the "Special Contribution Award."

His short *Taiwan from the Air* is released.

Creates personal short for Google: "Google Search Searching Story—Chi Po-lin."

2013   *Beyond Beauty: Taiwan from Above* is given a theatrical release, earning NT$220 million.

Beyond Beauty: Taiwan from Above wins Golden Horse for Best Documentary.

Taiwan National Parks from Above wins a gold at the 46th WorldFest-Houston International Film Festival.

My Heart, My Eyes, Seeing Taiwan: Chi Po-Lin's 20 Years of Perseverance and Affection is released.

Makes *Flying Over Kaohsiung* for the Urban Development Bureau of the Kaohsiung City Government.

Makes *Taichung: The Heart of Taiwan* for the Taichung City Government Information Bureau.

2014   Beyond Beauty: Taiwan from Above wins a Golden Sun at the 21st International Environmental Film Festival.

Beyond Beauty wins a special jury prize for creative excellence and a gold medal for cinematography at the 47th WorldFest-Houston International Film Festival.

Works with Forward Music to create a "*Beyond Beauty* Cross-Disciplinary Concert."

Works with the ROC's Air Rescue Group to create the short Beyond *Beauty: Taiwan's Merciful Airborne Angels*.

Is named "Taiwan Explorer" by National Geographic.

2015   Earns "King of Photography" honor at the "Power of the Image" international photography exhibition in Datong, China.

Makes *Seeing Taoyuan* for the Taoyuan City Government's Department of Agriculture.

2016   Wins an award for "Outstanding Contributions to the Arts" from the ROC military.

Personal short "Home Run Taiwan" is released.

2017   Holds press conference on June 8 about shooting the sequel to *Beyond Beauty: Taiwan from Above*.

Dies in a helicopter crash while shooting footage for the sequel in Hualien on June 10.

Earns a posthumous presidential citation on June 24.

A short film about him —"ZEISS Visionaries: Chi Po-lin"—is released.

Establishment of Chi Po-lin Foundation.

2019   Inauguration of Chi Po-lin Museum.

個展

2004 　　　「上天下地看台灣——台灣土地故事影像特展」，國立自然科學博物館戶外攝影展。

2005 　　　「上天下地看台灣——台灣土地故事影像特展」，中正紀念堂廣場舉辦，台灣最大規模戶外攝影展。

2010 　　　「正負 2 度 C 飛閱台灣」空中攝影展覽，台灣文創基金會。

2012 　　　「飛閱台灣 空拍環境影像展」，國立台灣科學教育館舉辦。

2016 　　　「看見・福爾摩沙空中攝影」公益巡迴展。

2017 　　　「飛閱台灣——齊柏林紀念攝影展」，台北少華山藝文空間、台北誠品信義店、
　　　　　　台中亞洲大學現代美術館、高雄駁二藝術特區。

2018 　　　「飛閱臺東 齊柏林」攝影展，國立臺灣圖書館、台中大墩文化中心。

出版

1999 　　　《上天下地看家園》空中攝影專輯。

2004 　　　《飛閱台灣：我們的土地故事》空中攝影專輯。

2005 　　　《悲歌美麗島》空中攝影專輯。

2006 　　　《從空中看台灣》齊柏林空中攝影專輯。

2008 　　　《台灣脈動》空中攝影作品合集發表於《經典》雜誌。

2014 　　　《鳥目台灣》攝影書，於香港發表。

2015 　　　《島嶼奏鳴曲》齊柏林空中攝影集。

2017 　　　《看見台灣 齊柏林的島嶼奏鳴曲》空中攝影集 於中國大陸發表。

2019 　　　《凝視 齊柏林：台灣的四維空間》。

作品典藏
國立臺灣美術館

Solo Exhibitions

2004   "Beyond Beauty: Seeing Taiwan from the Sky—An Exhibit of Images about the Land of Taiwan" at the National Museum of Natural Science.

2005   "Beyond Beauty: Seeing Taiwan from the Sky—An Exhibit of Images about the Land of Taiwan" at the Chiang Kai-shek Memorial's Liberty Square.
        (The largest outdoor photo exhibition in Taiwan's history.)

2010   "2 Degrees Celsius: An Aerial View of Taiwan," a photographic exhibit by the Taiwan Cultural & Creativity Development Foundation.

2012   "Our Land, Our Story," an exhibition of aerial photography at the National Taiwan Science Education Center.

2016   "Seeing Formosa: Aerial Photography," a public-interest traveling exhibition.

2017   "Taiwan from Above: An Exhibition in Commemoration of Chi Po-lin"—Taipei's Huashan 1914 Creative Park, Eslite's at Taipei Xinyi Branch,
        Asia University Museum of Modern Art in Taichung, and the Pier 2 Art Center in Kaohsiung.

2018   "Taitung from Above: Chi Po-lin," a photography exhibition at the National Taiwan Library and Taichung City's Dadun Cultural Center.

Publications

1999   *Our Land from Above*, a collection of aerial photography.

2004   *Our Land, Our Story*, a collection of aerial photography.

2005   *Elegy of a Beautiful Isle*, a collection of aerial photography.

2006   *Taiwan Aerial Imaging*, a collection of Chi Po-lin's aerial photography.

2008   *The Pulse of Taiwan*, a collection of aerial photography published by Rhythms Monthly.

2014   *Bird's Eye View of Taiwan*, a book of photographs published in Hong Kong.

2015   *Beyond Beauty: Taiwan from Above*, a collection of Chi Po-lin's aerial photography.

2017   *Beyond Beauty: Taiwan from Above*, a collection of aerial photographs published in mainland China.

2019   *In Focus: Chi Po-lin and Taiwan's Four-Dimensional Spacetime*, a collection of photography.

Museum Collections of his work:
National Taiwan Museum of Fine Art

凝視 齊柏林 ： 台灣的四維空間

作　　　者｜齊柏林
圖 片 撰 文｜張念中
翻　　　譯｜Jonathan Barnard（柏松年）

出　　　版｜財團法人看見·齊柏林基金會
總 編 輯｜萬冠麗
執 行 總 監｜黃寶琴
審 片 委 員｜陳郁文、陳其輝、黃烈文、黃寶琴、張育銘
編 輯 小 組｜李儒林、李欣彤、陳宣穎、詹宇雯（按姓氏筆劃）
美 術 設 計｜黃寶琴
中 英 校 對｜廖宏霖、黃亮榮、游牧笛、看見·齊柏林基金會 編輯小組
行 銷 企 劃｜蔡季芬、曾郁惠
發 行 服 務｜楊新玲、黃紹榮
校色·印刷｜優秀視覺設計有限公司

財團法人看見·齊柏林基金會｜Chi Po-lin Foundation
T - (886-2) 2933-0994　　　F - (886-2) 2629-5840
A - 25158 新北市淡水區中正路 298 號 2 樓
W - https://www.chipolin.org

初 版 一 刷｜　2019 年 12 月
定　　　價｜　新台幣 1980 元
I S B N　　｜　978-986-97745-1-2（精裝）

本攝影集採用：源圓紙業· 九八超雪 180 G

國家圖書館出版品預行編目 (CIP) 資料

凝視 齊柏林：台灣的四維空間 / 齊柏林攝影.
-- 初版 . -- 臺北市：看見 · 齊柏林基金會, 2019.11
　218 面 ； 29x28 公分 .
ISBN 978-986-97745-1-2(精裝)

733.3　　　108019209

1. 齊柏林　2. 台灣　3. 土地　4. 自然　5. 空拍